Belleville Ontario Book 4 in Colour Photos, Saving Our History One Photo at a Time

Photography
by Barbara Raué
2016

Series Name:
Cruising Ontario

Book 166: Belleville Book 4

Cover photo: 70 Bridge Street West, Page 33

Series Name: Cruising Ontario
Saving Our History One Photo at a Time
in colour photos

Books Available in Alphabetical Order:
Aberfoyle, Acton, Alton, Amherstburg, Ancaster, Arthur, Aylmer, Ayr, Bloomingdale, Brantford, Burlington, Caledon, Caledonia, Cambridge, Clifford, Conestogo, Delhi, Dorchester to Aylmer, Drayton, Drumbo, Dundas, Eden Mills, Elmira, Elora, Essex, Fergus, Guelph, Hagersville, Hamilton, Hanover, Harriston, Hespeler, Jarvis, Kingston, Kingsville, Kitchener, Linwood, Listowel, London, Lucknow, Mono, Mount Forest, Neustadt, New Hamburg, Niagara-on-the-Lake, Oakville, Orangeville, Orillia, Owen Sound, Palmerston, Peterborough, Petrolia, Port Elgin, Preston, Rockwood, Sarnia, Seaforth, Sheffield, Shelburne, Simcoe, Southampton, St. Jacobs, St. Marys, St. Thomas, Stoney Creek, Stratford, Thamesford, Tillsonburg, Waterdown, Waterford, Waterloo, Welland, Wellesley, Windsor, Wingham, Woodstock

Other Books by Barbara Raue

Coins of Gold

Arrows, Indians and Love

The Life and Times of Barbara
Volume 1: Inventions That Have Enhanced My Life
Volume 2: Entertainment That I Have Enjoyed
Volume 3: East Coast Trips
Volume 4: Olympics Have Always Intrigued Me
Volume 5: Wonders of the World
Volume 6: Caribbean Cruises We Have Enjoyed
Volume 7: Animals
Volume 8: Storms and Other Major Disasters in My Lifetime
Volume 9: Wars, Terrorist Attacks and Major Disasters

The Cromwell Family Book

Laura Secord Discovered

Daddy Where Are You?

Montana Series
Book 1: Montana Dream
Book 2: Life on the Montana Frontier
Book 3: Montana to Boston and Back

Visit Barbara's website to view all of her books
http://barbararaue.ca

Table of Contents

Belleville is a city located at the mouth of the Moira River on the Bay of Quinte in southeastern Ontario. It was the site of a Mississaugas' village in the eighteenth century. It was settled by United Empire Loyalists beginning in 1784. It was named Belleville in honor of Lady Arabella Gore in 1816, after a visit to the settlement by Sir Francis Gore and his wife.

It is known as the "friendly city" because it offers big city amenities along with small town friendliness, and a pleasing mixture of the historic and modern.

Belleville became an important railway junction with the completion of the Grand Trunk Railway in 1855. In 1858 the iron bridge over the Moira River at Bridge Street was constructed. Belleville's beautiful High Victorian Gothic city hall was built in 1872 to house the public market and administrative offices.

Due to its location near Lake Ontario, its climate is moderated by cooling hot summer days and warming cold days during the fall and winter.

Procter & Gamble, Kellogg's, Redpath, and Sears are corporations operating in Belleville. There are many other manufacturing sector companies which operate within the City of Belleville, including Sprague Foods, Sigma Stretch Film Canada, Reid's Dairy, and Parmalat Canada - Black Diamond Cheese Division, to name a few.

Belleville has an excellent yacht harbor, which is a picturesque stopping point for Great Lakes sailors and a favorite launch for sports fishing enthusiasts after walleye, pike and bass. Beautiful music chimes can be heard all year long from the City Hall clock tower, overlooking the new civic square and Farmers Market. Walking, biking and rollerblading can be enjoyed on the Bayshore and Riverfront Trails.

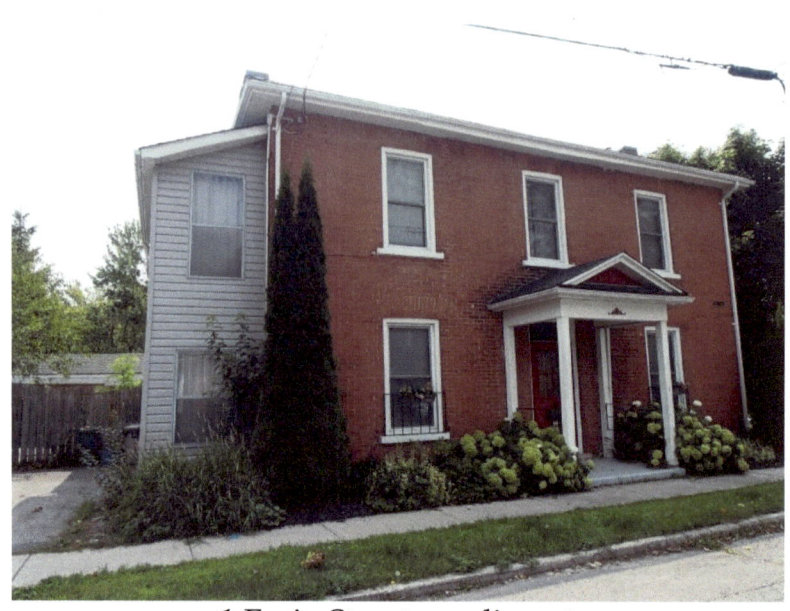

1 Forin Street - pediment

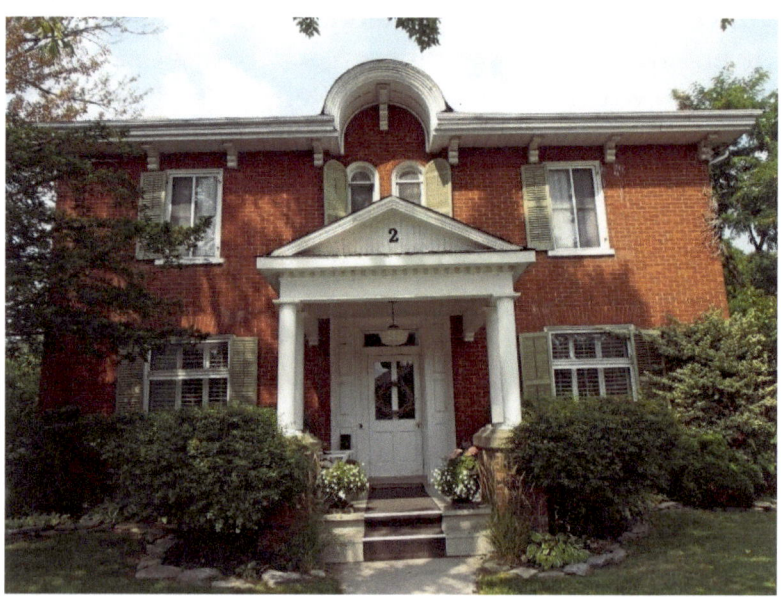

2 Forin Street – cornice brackets, pediment, transom window above door

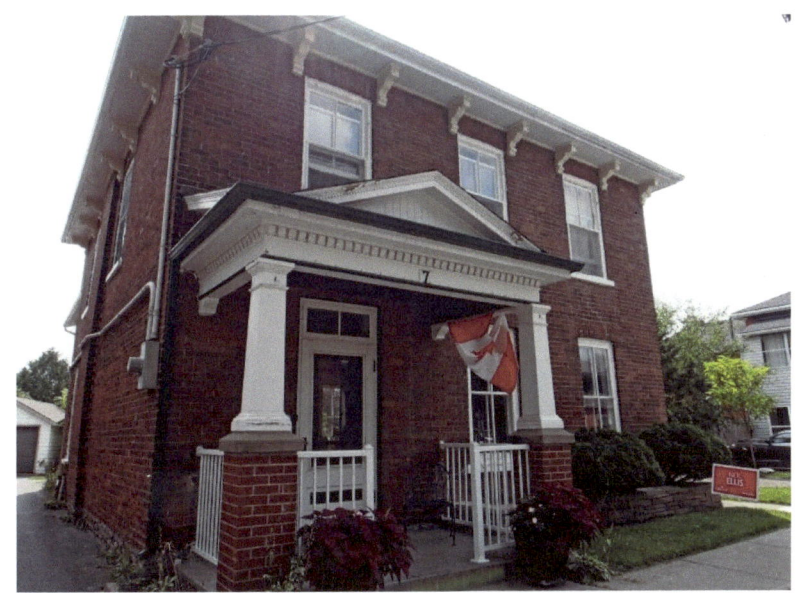

7 Forin Street - cornice brackets, pediment, dentil molding, transom window above door

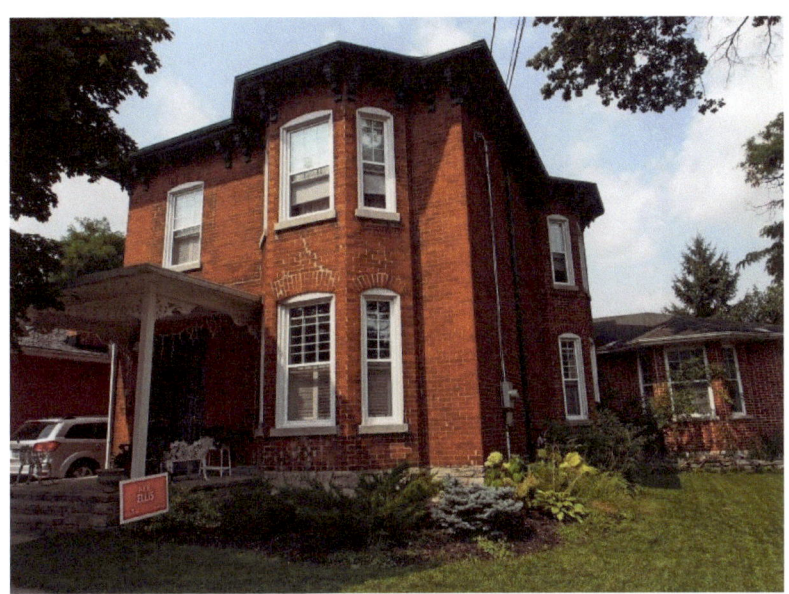

10 Forin Street – two-storey bay window, cornice brackets

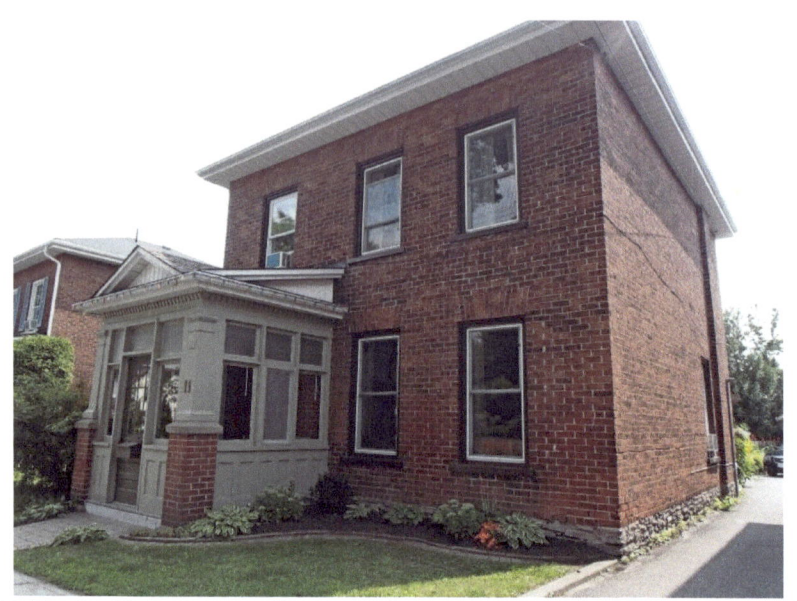

11 Forin Street – pediment above enclosed entrance porch

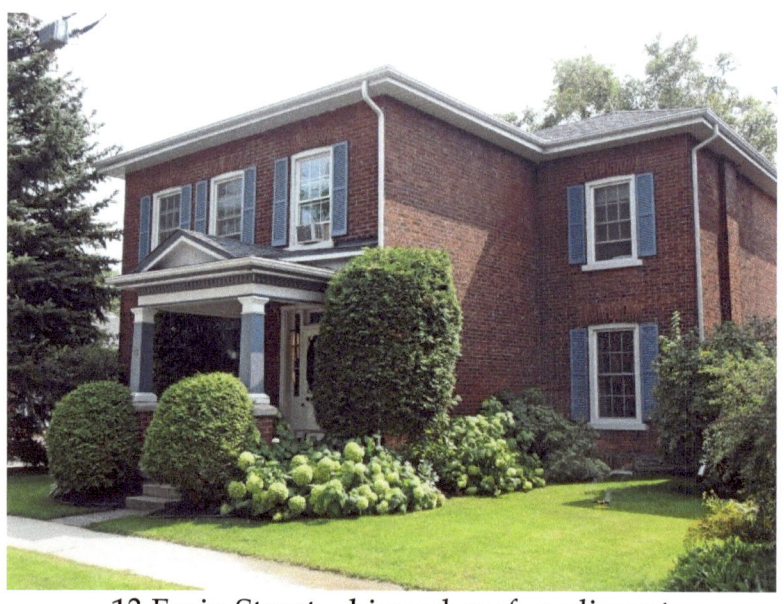

13 Forin Street – hipped roof, pediment

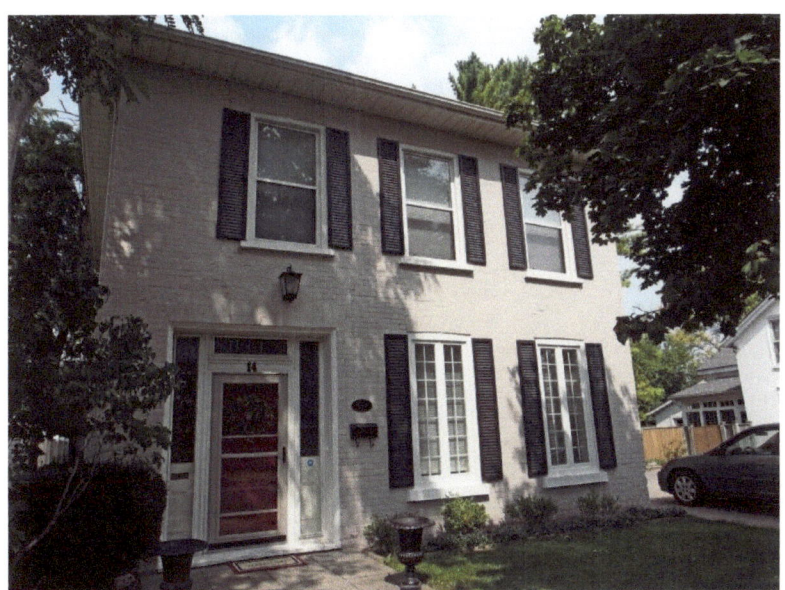

14 Forin Street

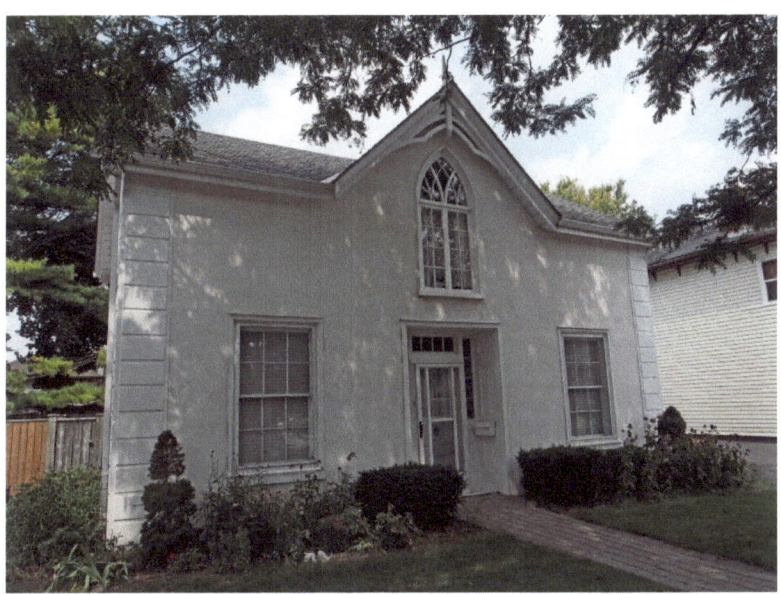

16 Forin Street – Gothic – verge board trim on gable, corner quoins, sidelights and transom window

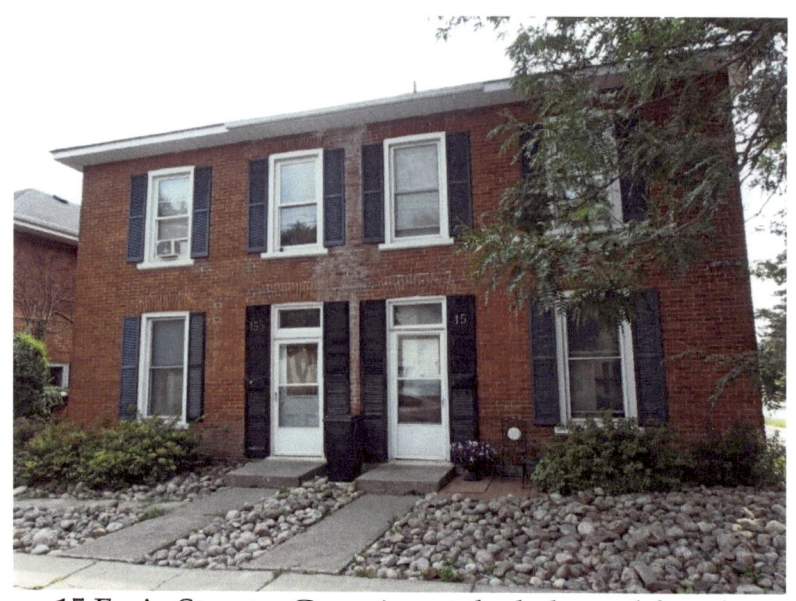

15 Forin Street – Georgian style, balanced façade

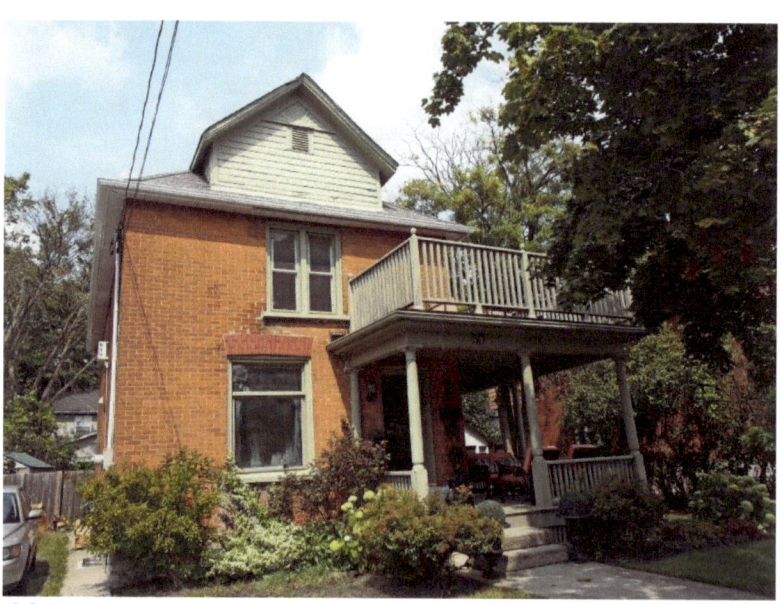

30 Forin Street – dormer in attic, second floor balcony

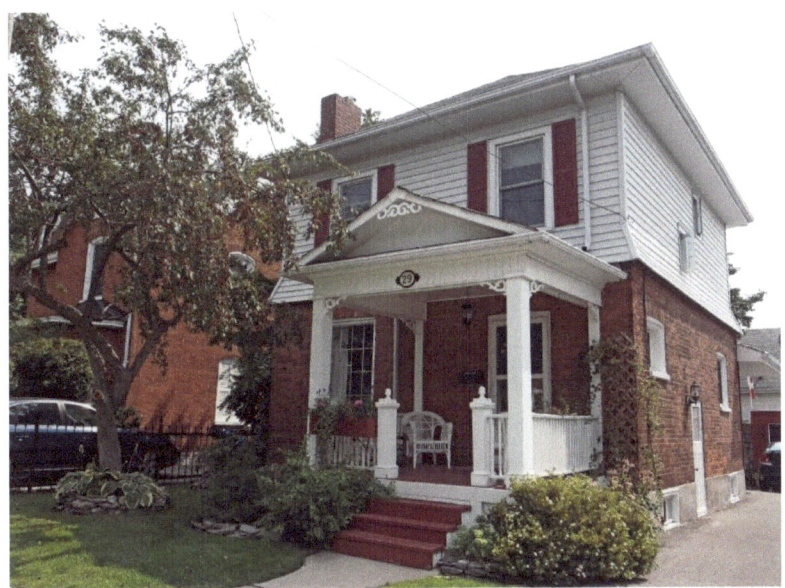

29 Forin Street – pediment, bric-a-brac on porch pillars

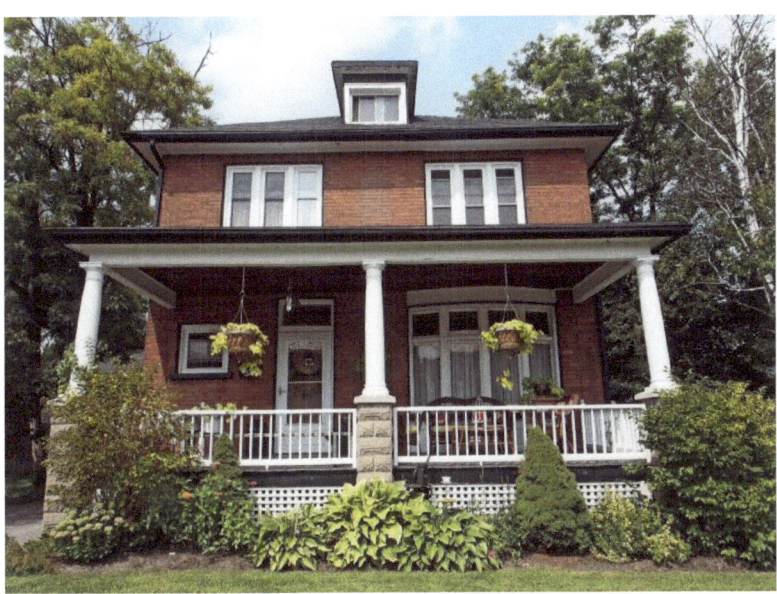

34 Forin Street – dormer in hipped roof, Doric pillars

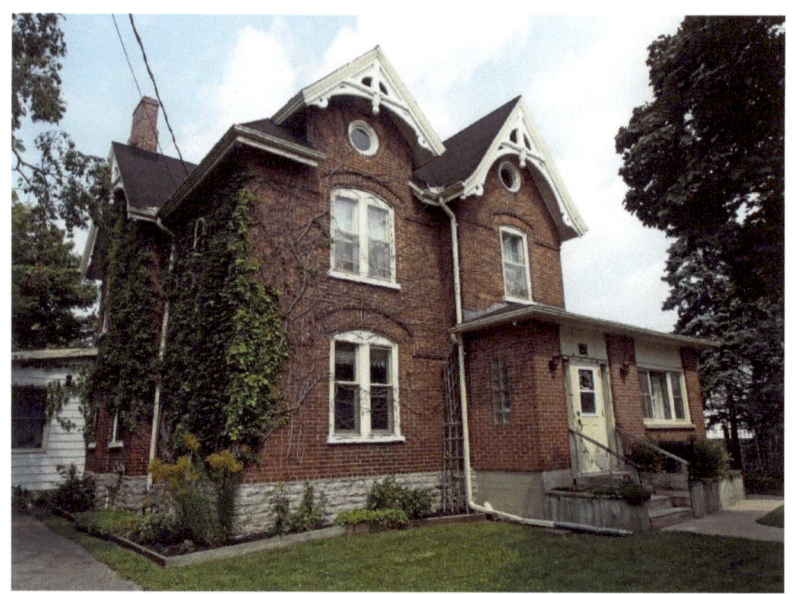

38 Forin Street – Gothic – verge board trim and finials on gables, round windows in gables, window voussoirs

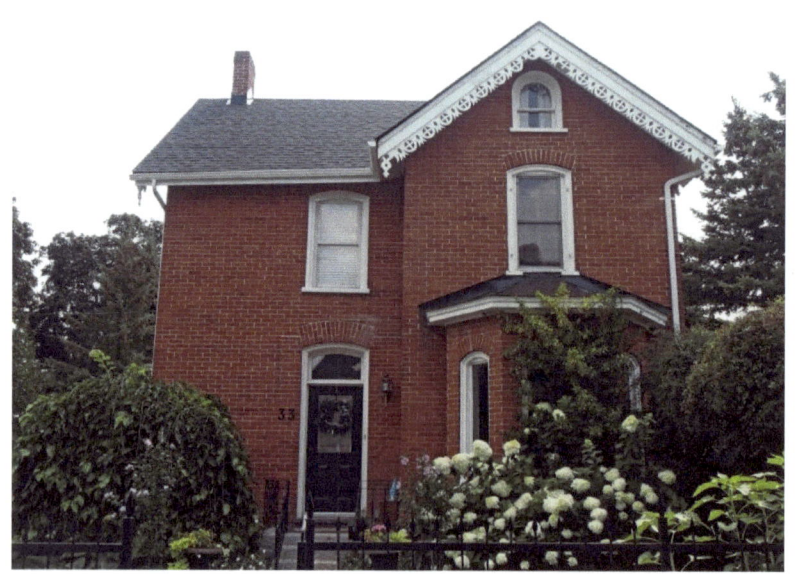

33 Forin Street – verge board trim on gable, bay window

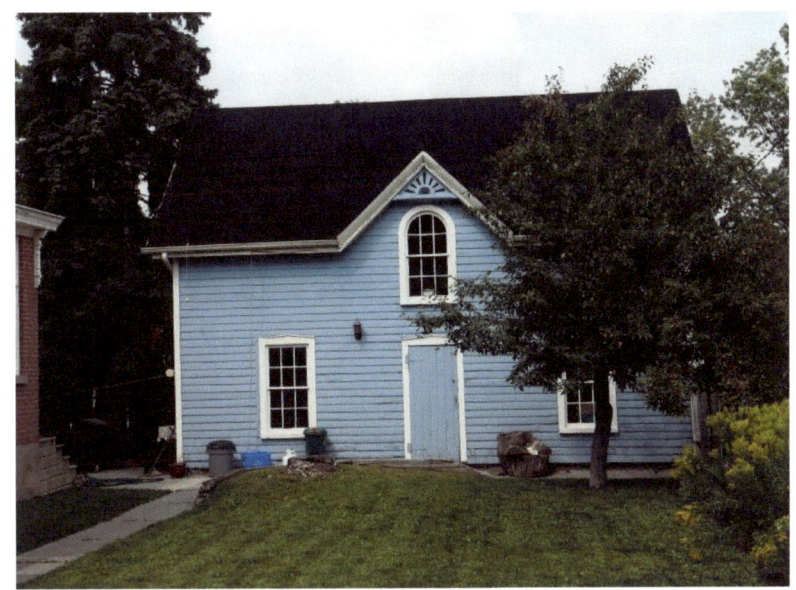

Forin Street – Ontario Cottage – verge board trim on peak of gable

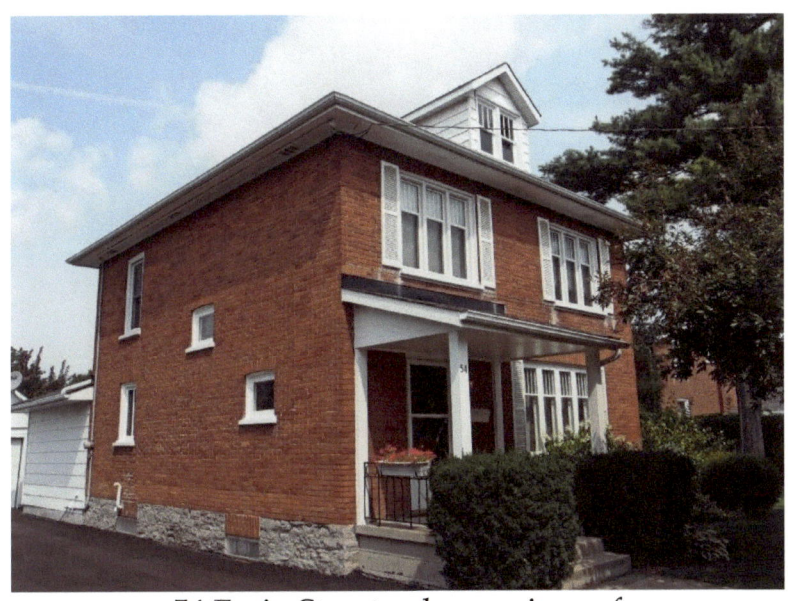

54 Forin Street – dormer in roof

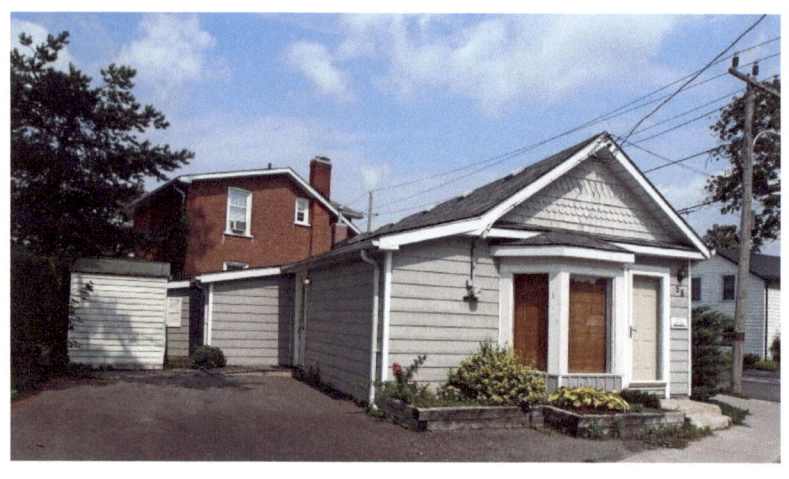

56 Forin Street – Langewisch Psychology Services

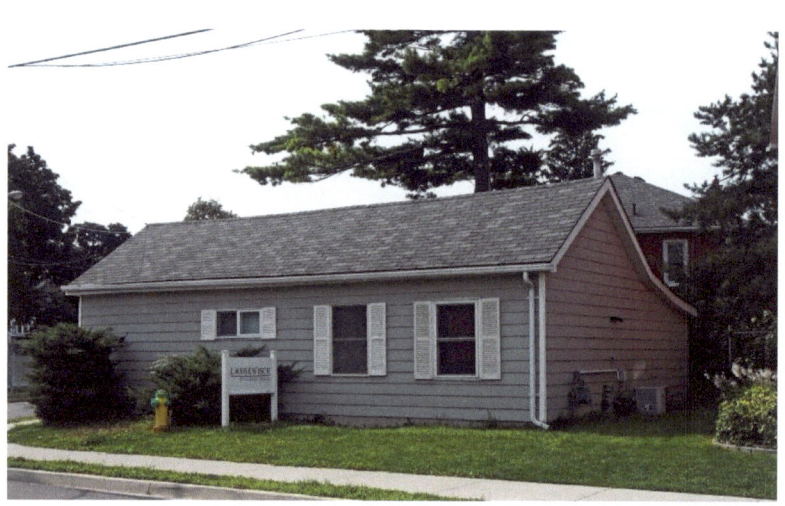

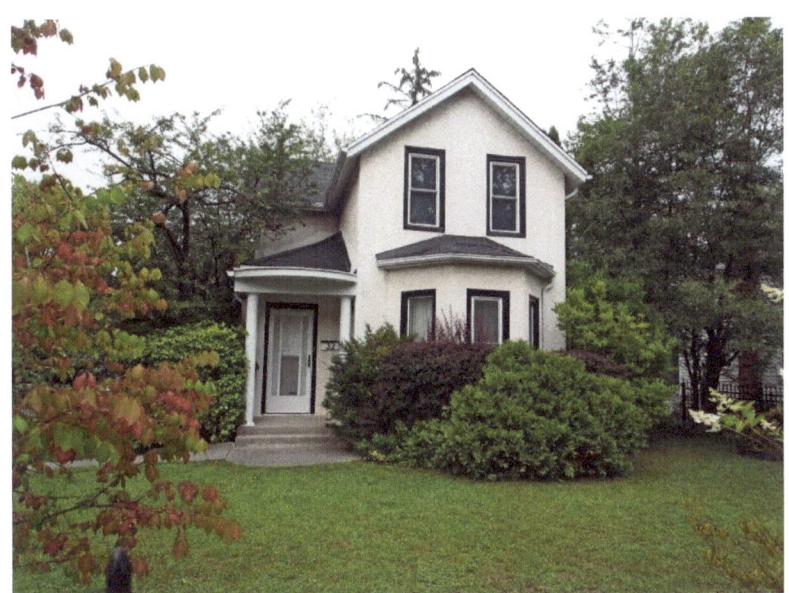

32 Mount Pleasant Road – Gothic, bay window

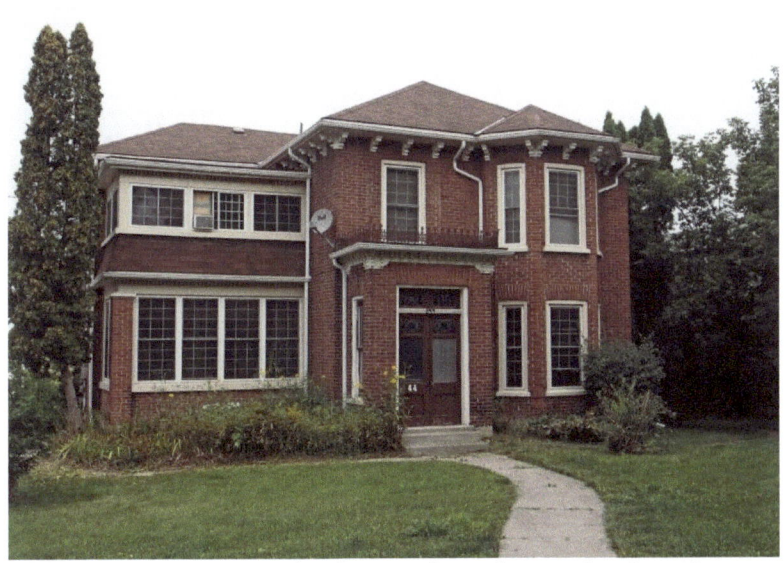

44 Mount Pleasant Road – hipped roof, cornice brackets, two-storey bay window, iron cresting above enclosed front porch

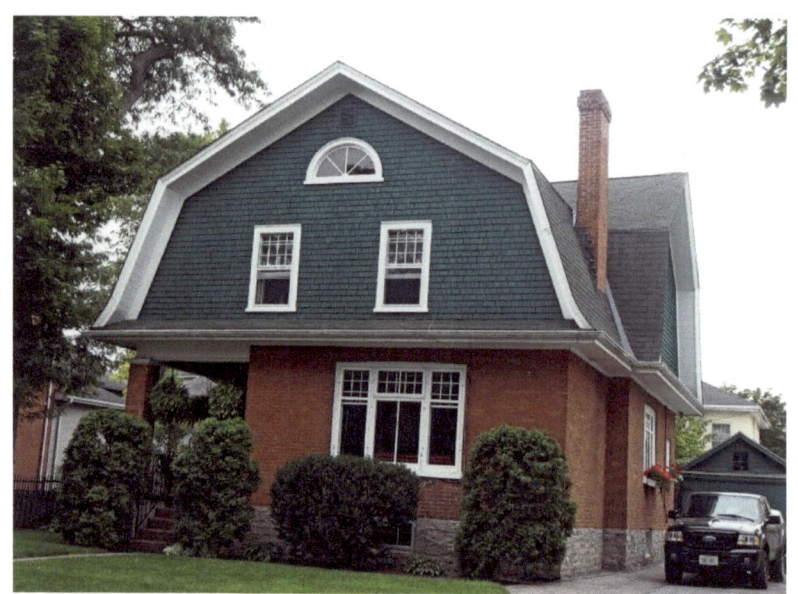

Mount Pleasant Road – Neo-colonial style – gambrel roof

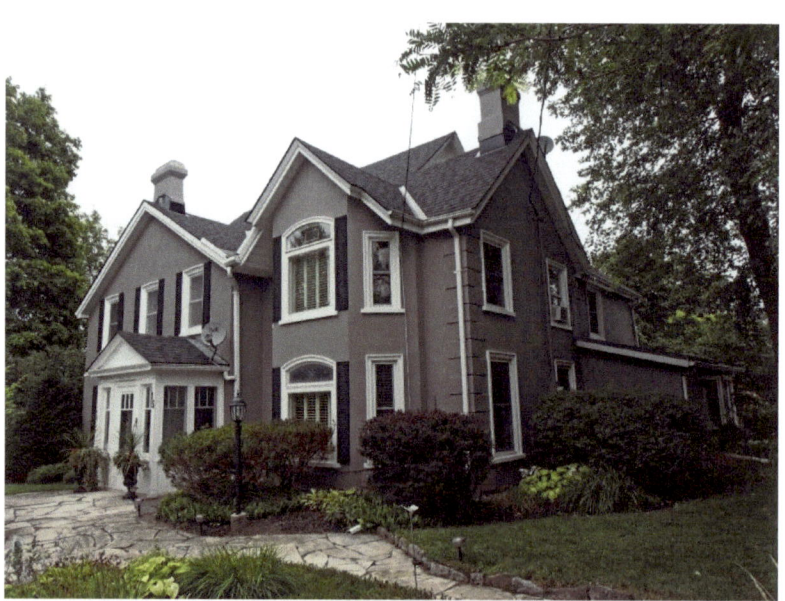

15 Mount Pleasant Road – Queen Anne style – corner quoins

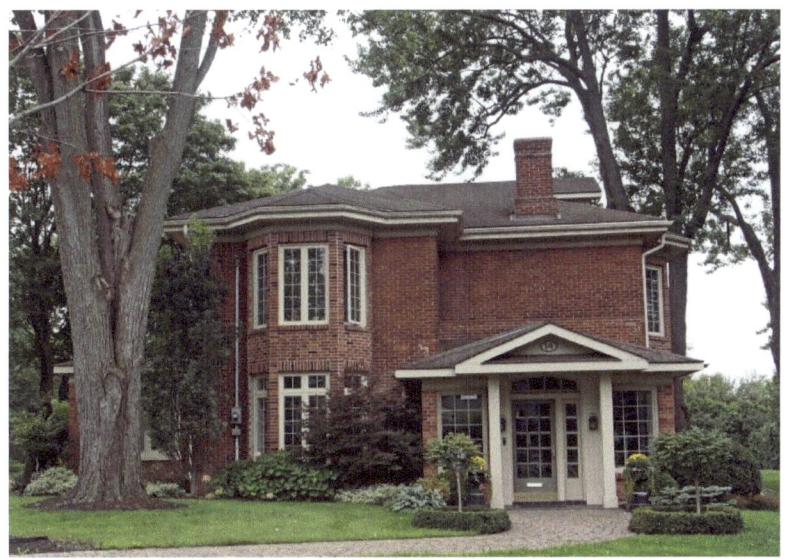

14 Mount Pleasant Road – hipped roof, two-storey bay window, pediment, sidelights and transom window

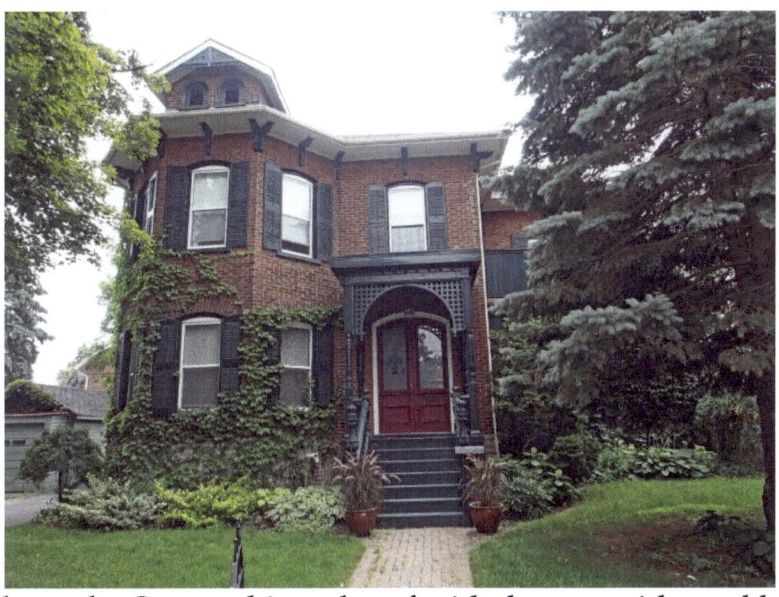

Alexander Street – hipped roof with dormer with a gabled roof and verge board trim and two windows; cornice brackets; two-storey bay window;

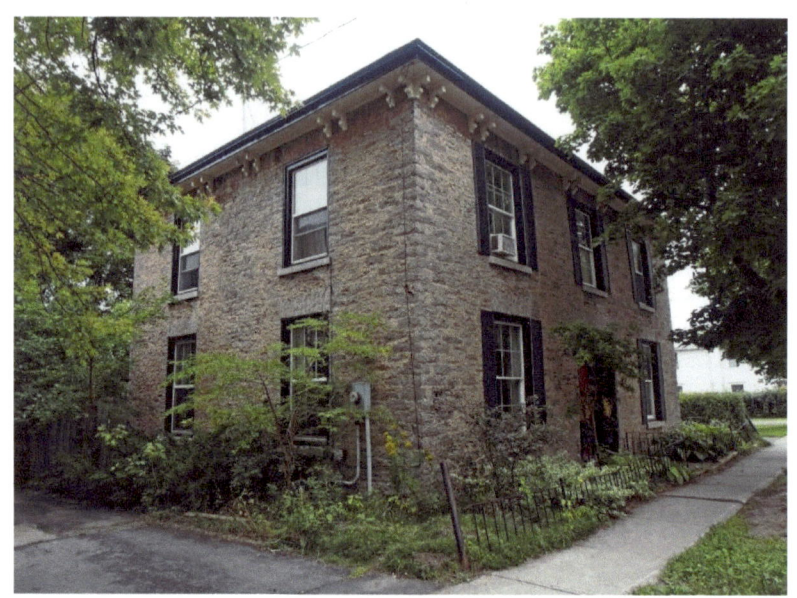

56 Alexander Street – stone building, paired cornice brackets

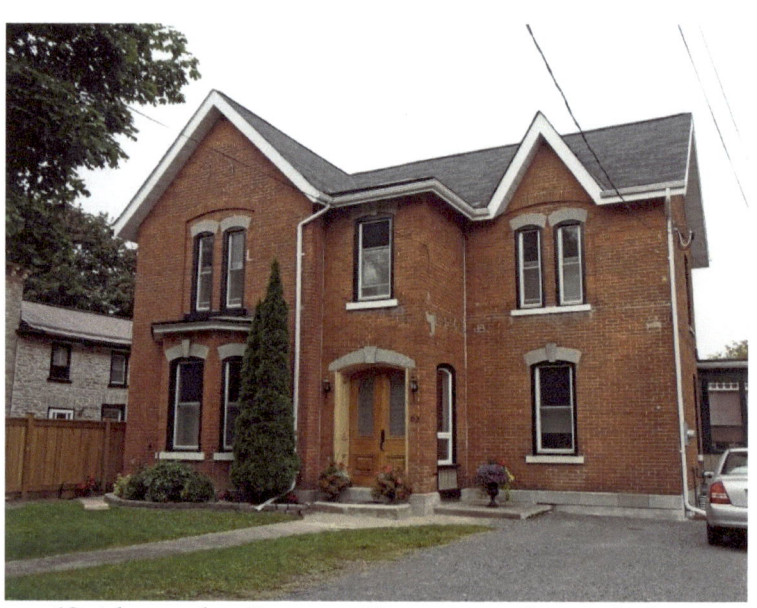

62 Alexander Street – Victorian – bay window

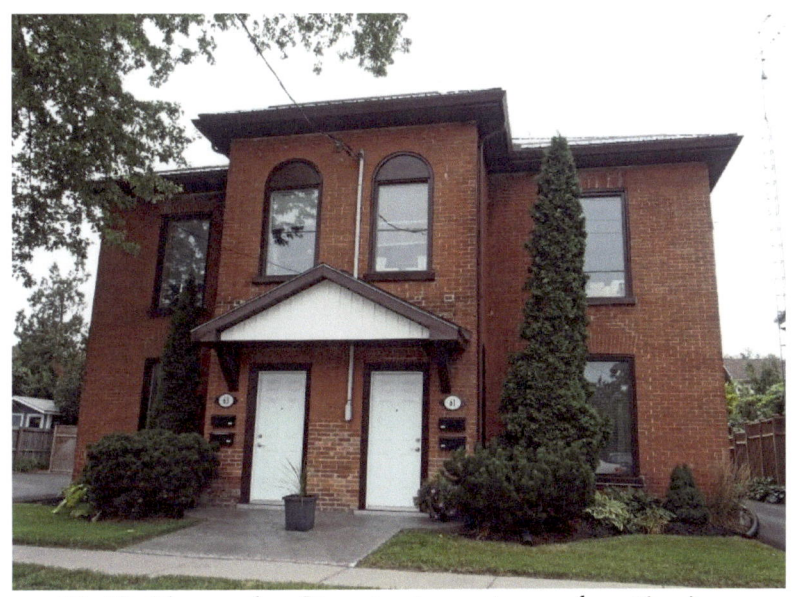

61-63 Alexander Street – two-storey frontispiece

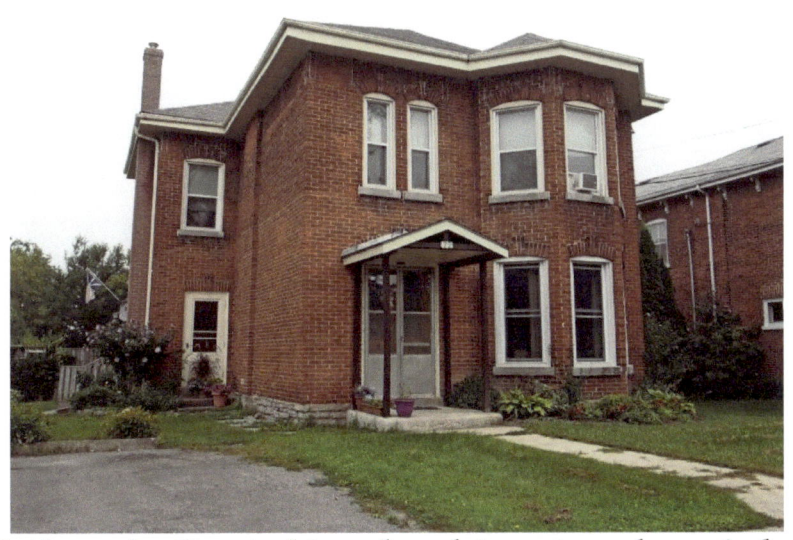

72 Alexander Street – hipped roof, two-storey bay window

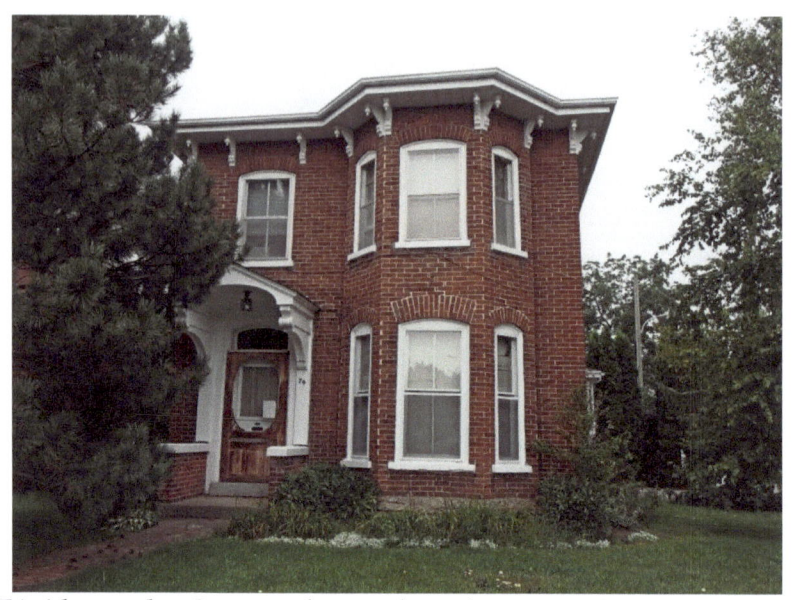

74 Alexander Street – hipped roof, cornice brackets, two-storey bay window, voussoirs

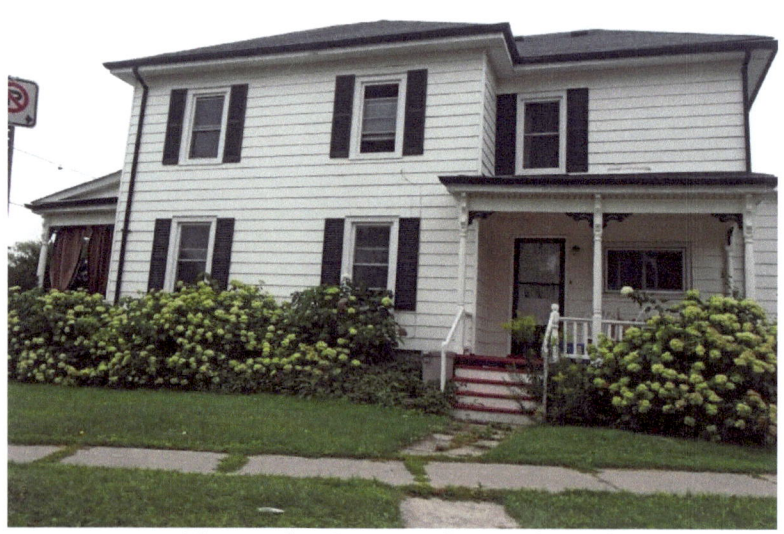

Alexander Street – hipped roof

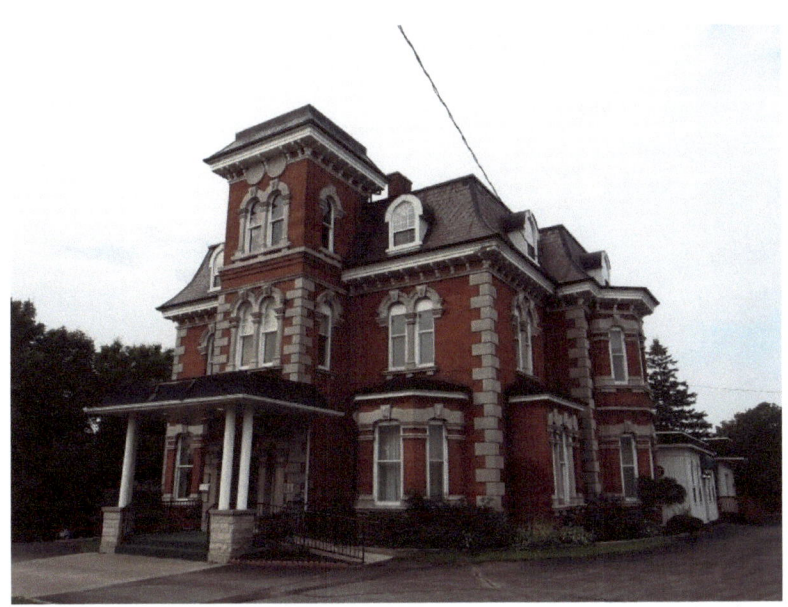

68 North Front Street – Belleville Funeral Home and Chapel -
a Victorian mansion – three storey tower; dichromatic corner
quoins; Mansard roof with dormers, prominent keystones,
drip molds and engaged columns; engaged columns at front
entrance with sidelights and transom window

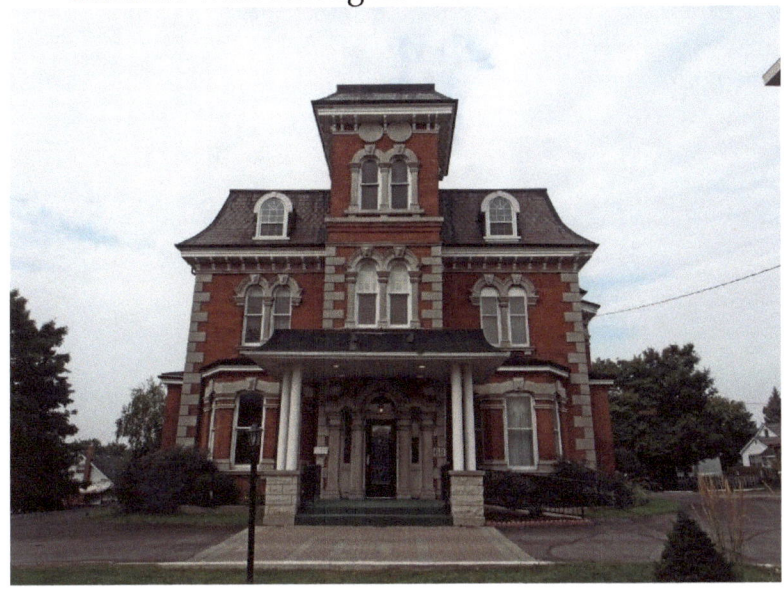

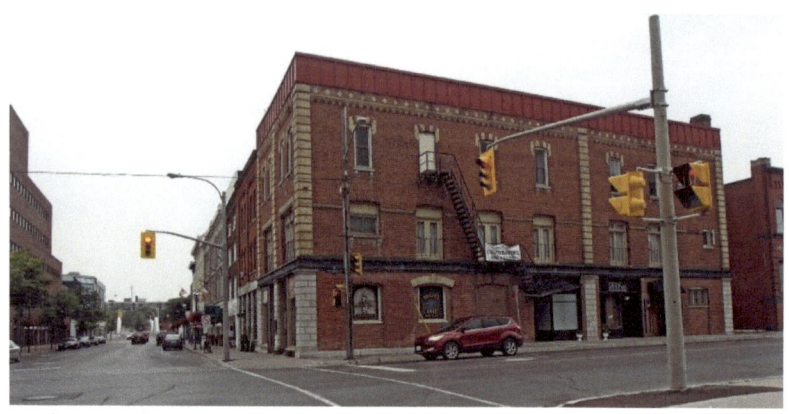

142 North Front Street at Pinnacle Street – John's Hair Quarters Barber Shop – dichromatic brickwork, corner quoins

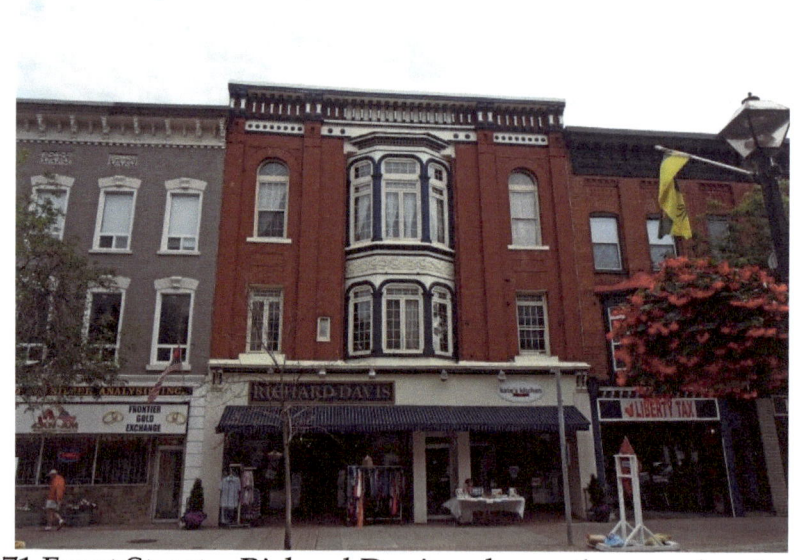

271 Front Street – Richard Davis – decorative cornice, two-storey bay windows, pilasters

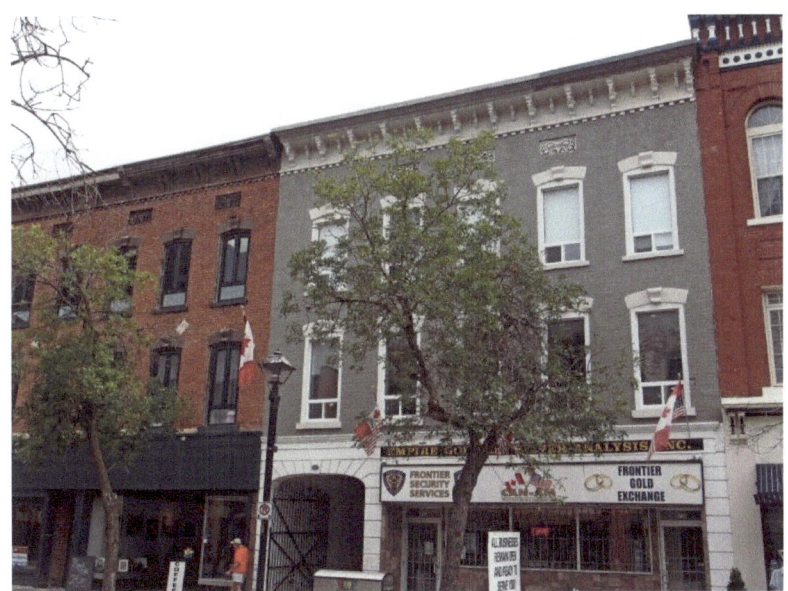

277 Front Street North – Frontier Gold Exchange – cornice brackets, decorative brickwork

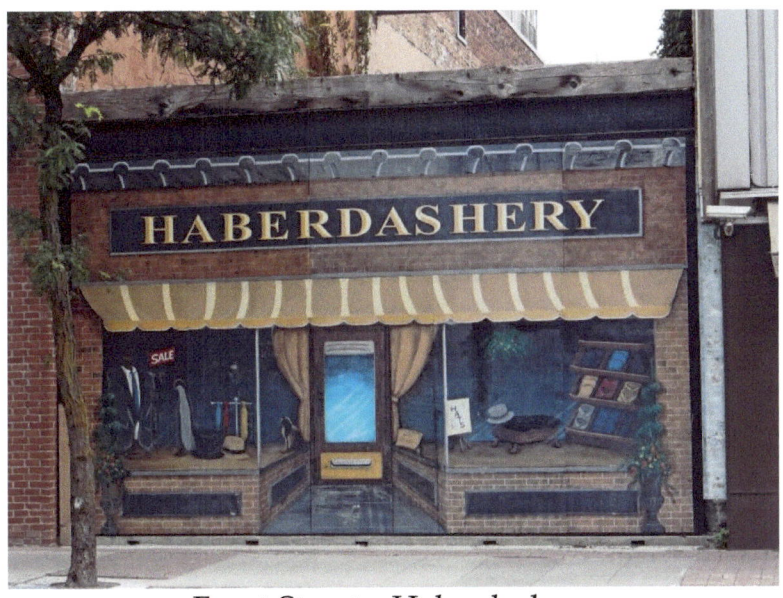

Front Street – Haberdashery

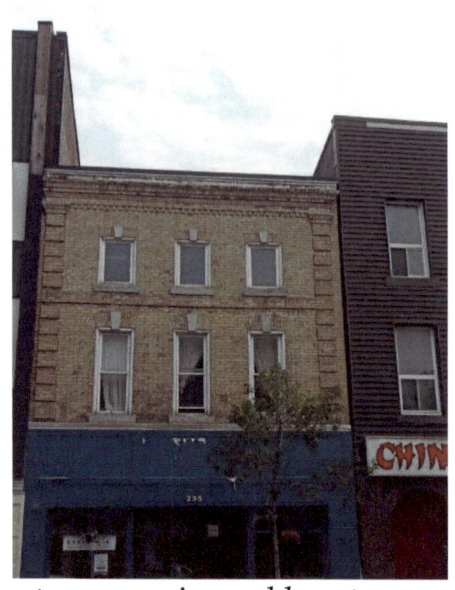

255 Front Street – voussoirs and keystones, corner quoins

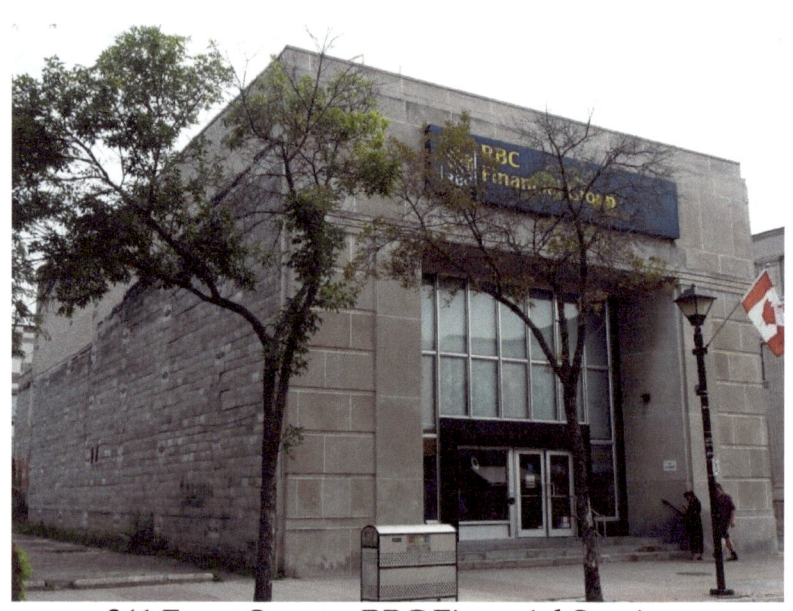

241 Front Street – RBC Financial Services

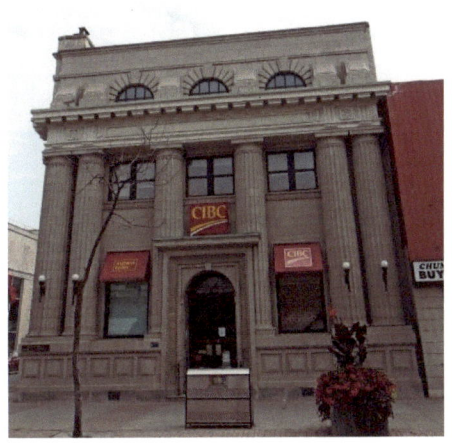

366 North Front Street at Campbell Street – CIBC - Beaux Arts style – engaged columns with Doric capitals, voussoirs and keystones

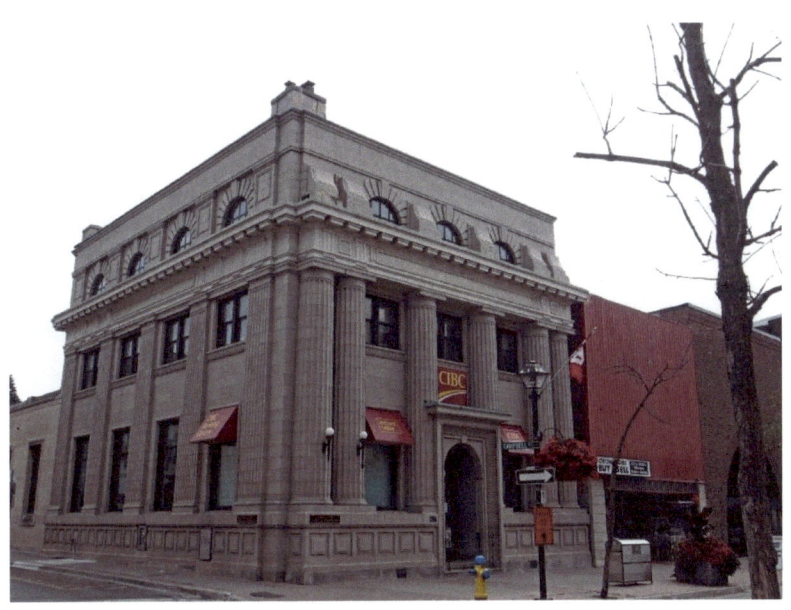

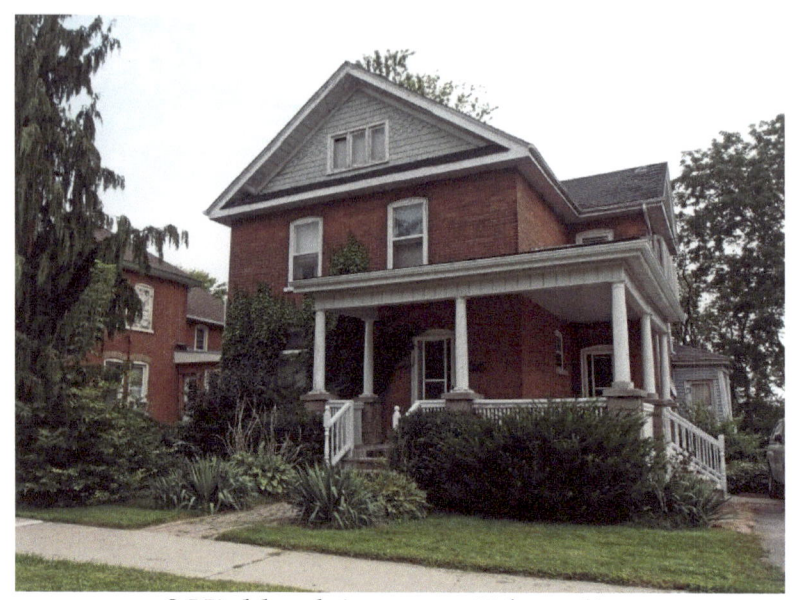

9 Highland Avenue – Edwardian

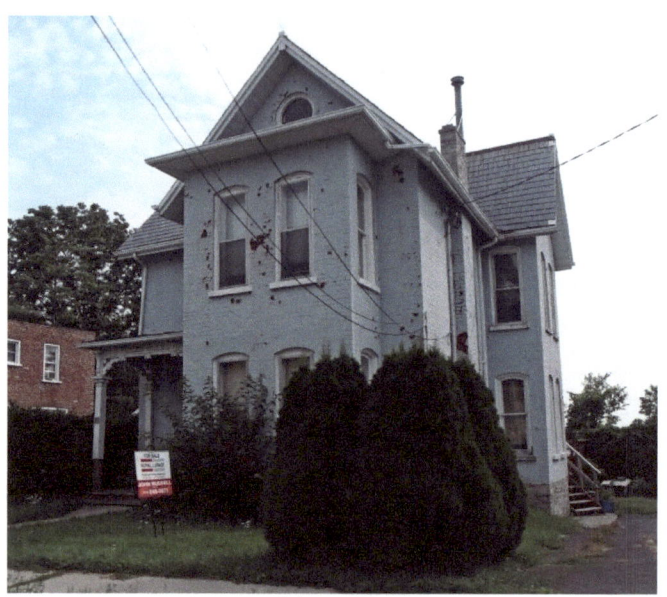

11 Highland Avenue

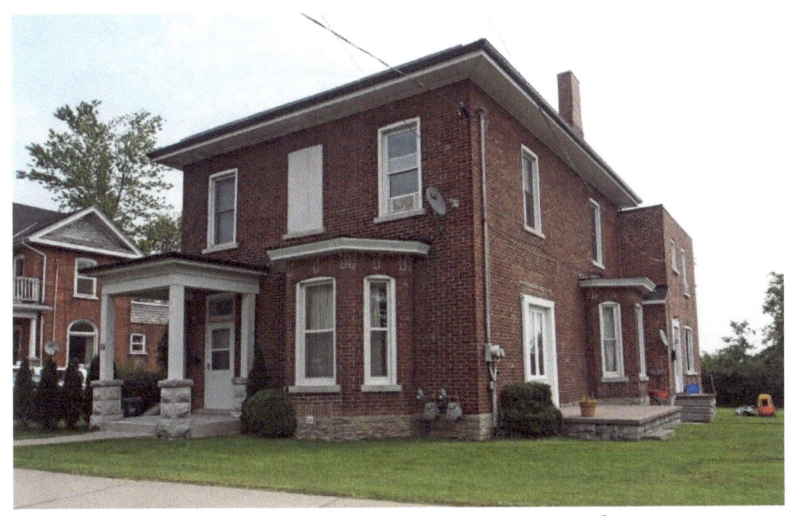

15 Highland Avenue – bay window

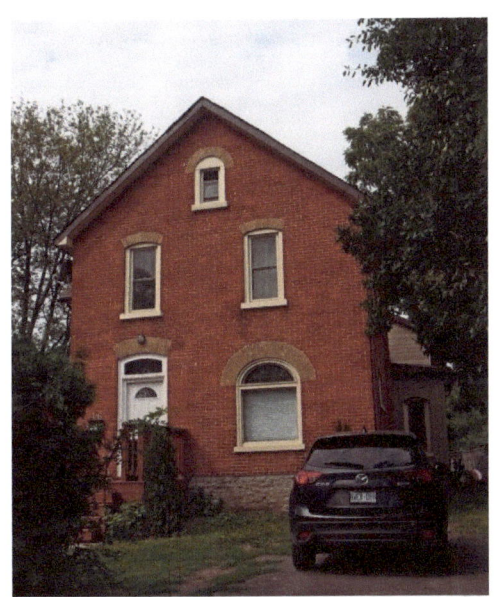

16 Highland Avenue – Gothic - voussoirs

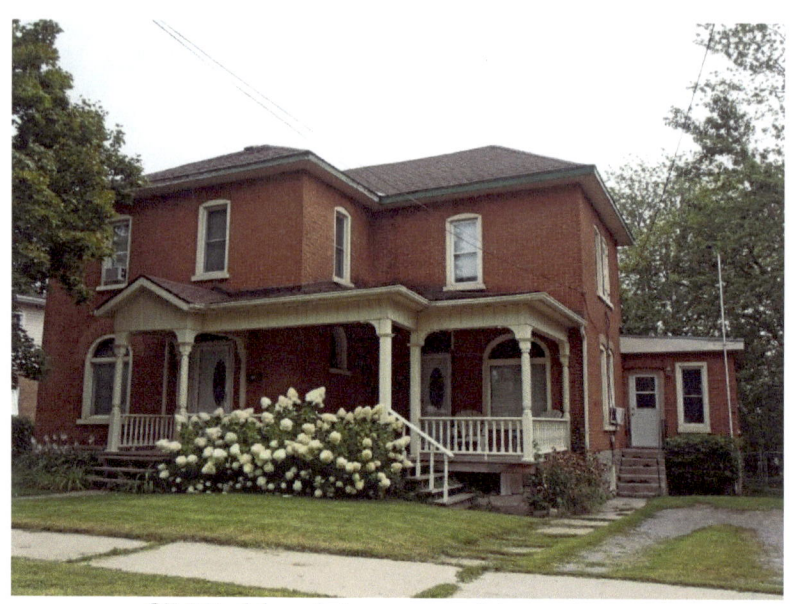

25 Highland Avenue – hipped roof

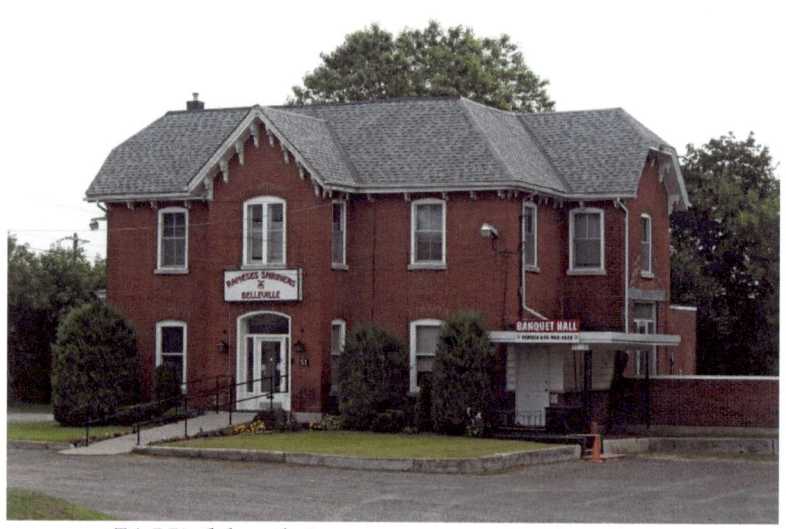

51 Highland Avenue – cornice brackets

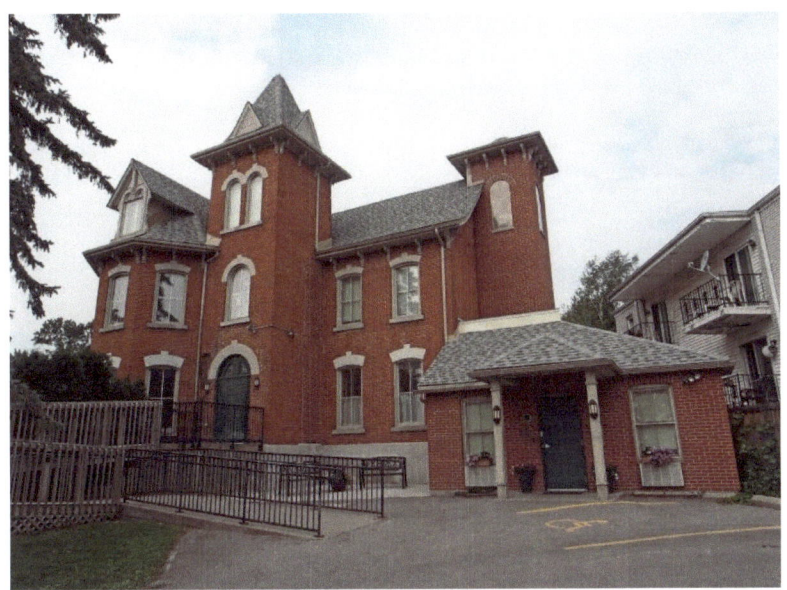

58 Highland Avenue – Queen Anne style – three-storey tower, turret, cornice brackets, voussoirs and keystones

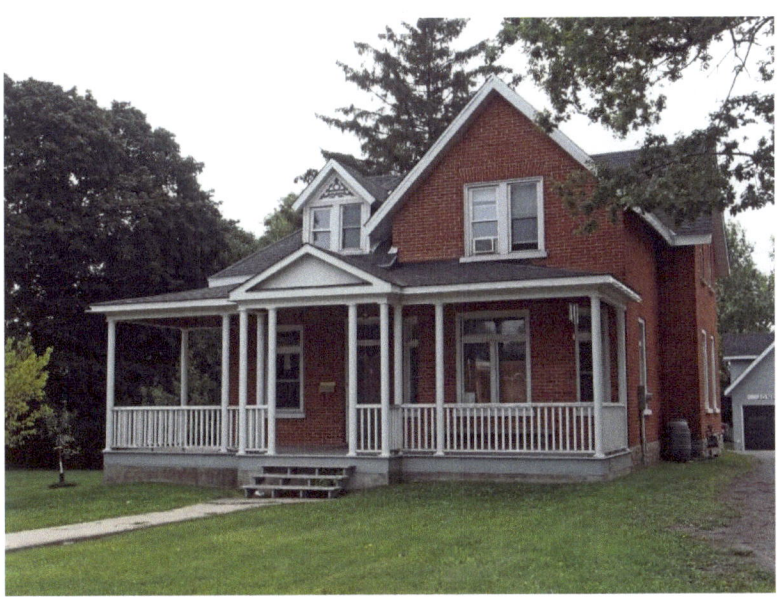

73 Highland Avenue – dormer, pediment

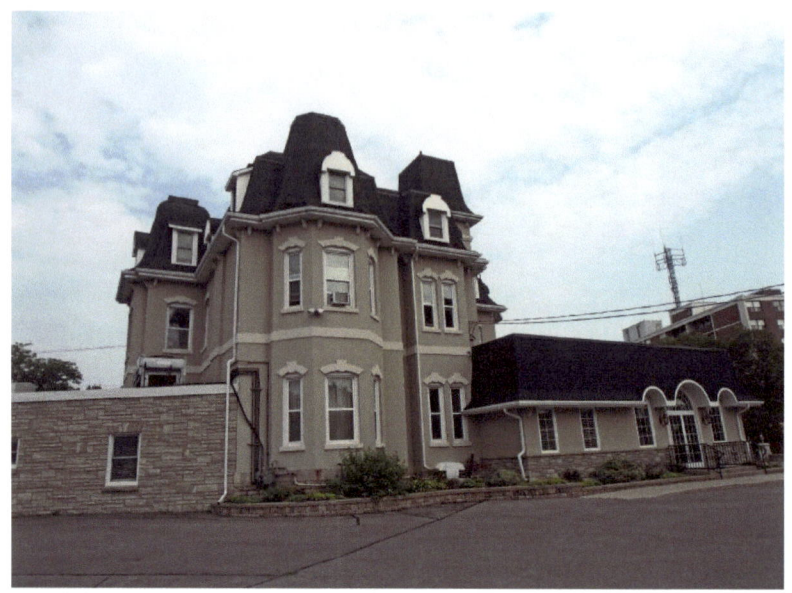

80 Highland Avenue – John R. Bush Funeral Home – Second Empire style – Mansard roof with dormers, cornice brackets, banding

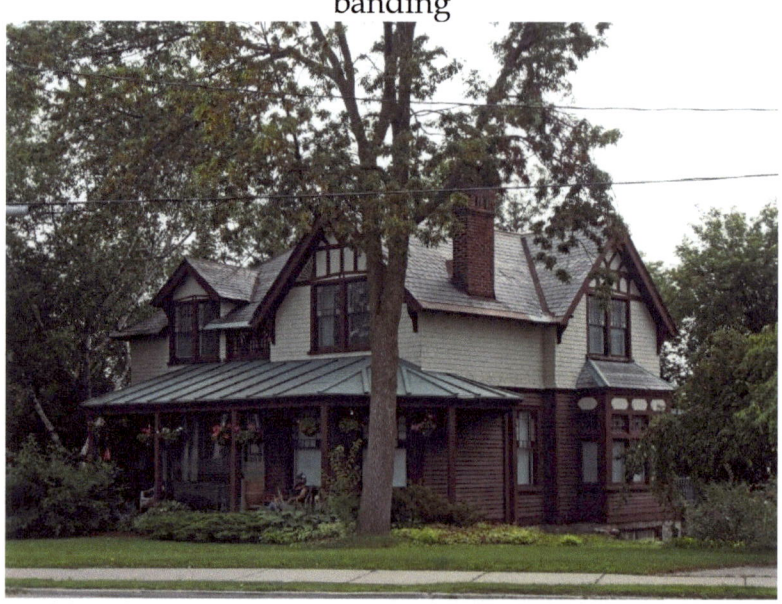

Highland Avenue – Tudor half-timbering in gables, bay window

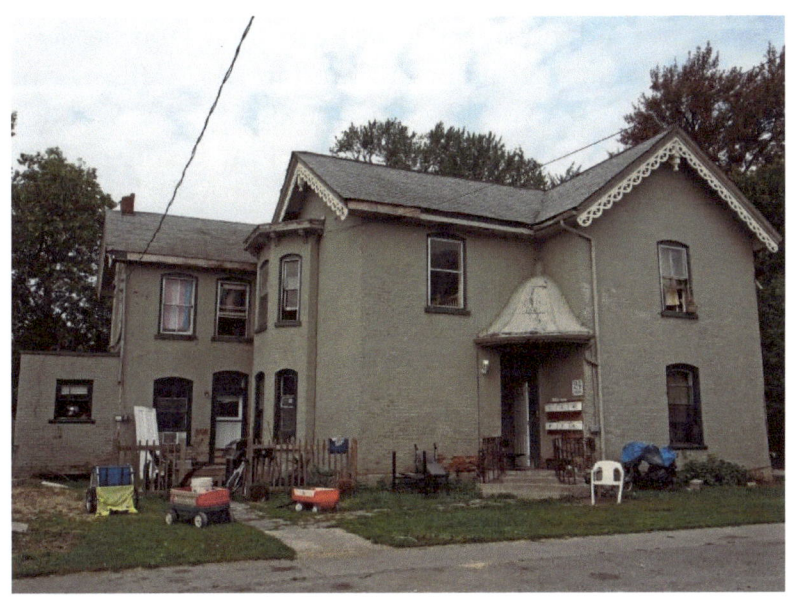

24 Dunbar Avenue

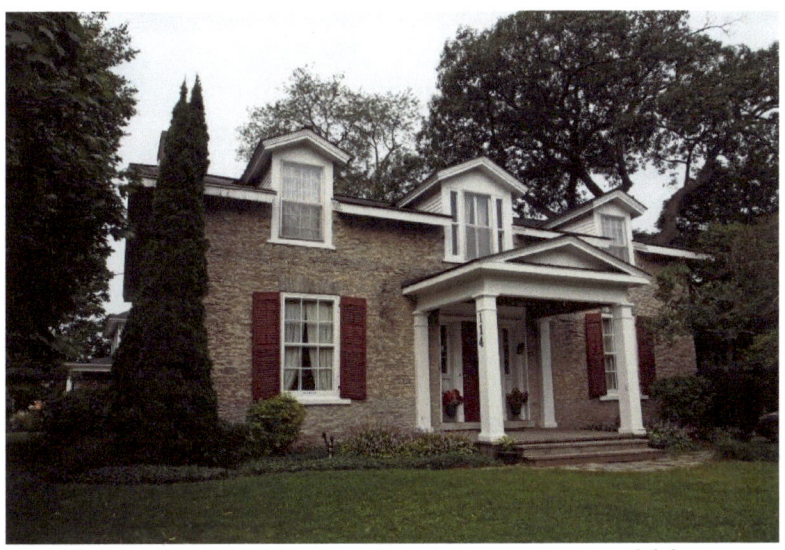

114 Bridge Street West at Sinclair Street – cobblestone, dormers, pediment, engaged columns beside door with sidelights - The Moodie cottage is marked with a heritage plaque at 114 Bridge Street West at Sinclair Street in Belleville.

Born in England in 1803, Mrs. Susanna Moodie emigrated to Canada with her husband in 1832. They farmed near Cobourg for two years and then moved to the wooded Rice Lake area near the frontier of the colony before settling in the more urban environment of Belleville in 1840. She became a leading author of the pre-Confederation period and her poems and short stories appeared in journals in Canada and England. Her two autobiographical books, *Roughing it in the Bush* (1852), and *Life in the Clearings* (1853) have become Canadian classics.

Roughing It In The Bush is about as Canadian a term as one can imagine. The bush is the bush, with tangled trees, voracious blackflies and slithery things in the swamp. Susanna Moodie wanted to get the point across to her middle-class friends in England and she wrote bluntly. Her book, first published in England in 1852, was a painful counterpoint to all the land agents' persuasive talk about Canada being a land of glorious opportunity.

Moodie moved to a sunnier spot in one of "the clearings", as she called it, Belleville. A clearing was an apt description, for if you can visualize the North America of the 1830s through a writer's imagination, you would see a vast endless carpet of forest, with occasional holes eaten in it as if by hungry moths. Those ragged spaces were created by settlements, such as Belleville at the mouth of the Moira River.

Before coming to Canada, Moodie had established herself as a writer in England. Her publishing connections served her well when she embarked on her Canadian literary career in the 1850s. Her books were published successfully in Britain and much later in Canada. Susanna wrote six books.

Life in the Belleville clearing was rough. One of their young sons drowned in the Moira River which ran beneath the hill not far from their home. Another was lost in childbirth.

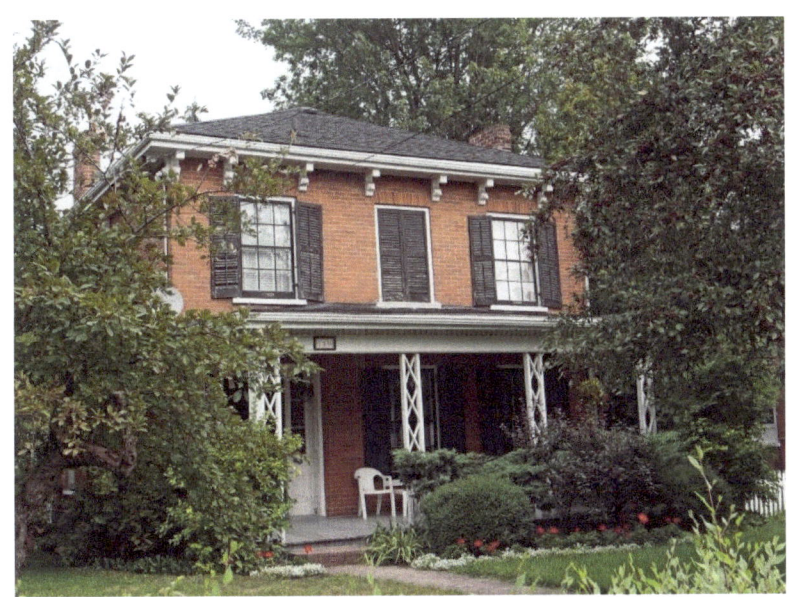

110 Bridge Street West – **built in** 1867 by Smith Steven, clerk in the Grand Trunk Railway solicitor's office - excellent example of a family home owner of modest means; has original 6/6 pane windows, window sills, and shutters; acorn brackets extend under the cornice; the front door has narrow sidelights

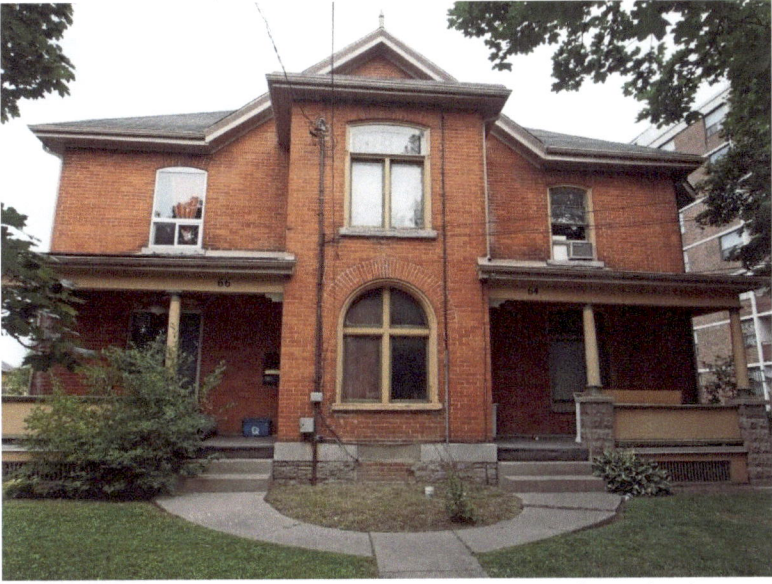

64-68 Bridge Street West – two-storey frontispiece

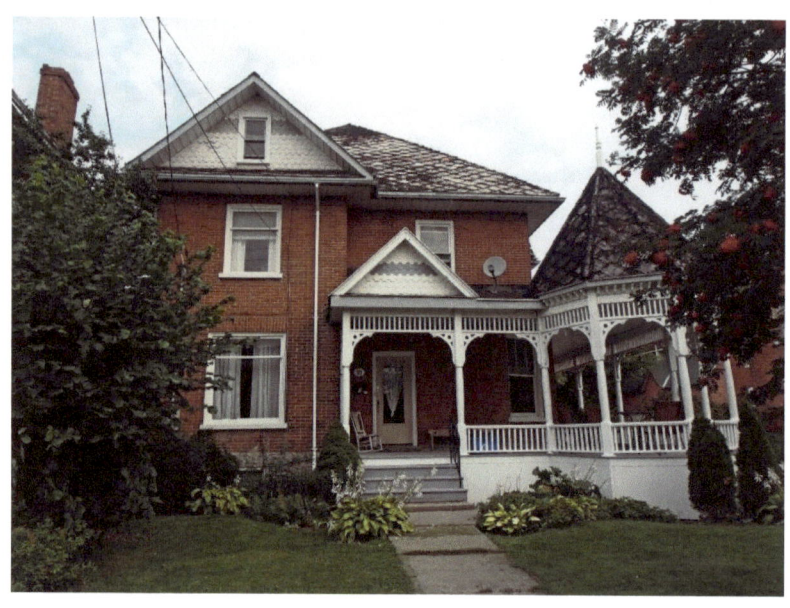

70 Bridge Street West – Victorian – ornate capitals on posts for wraparound veranda, cone-shaped cap on corner, pediment

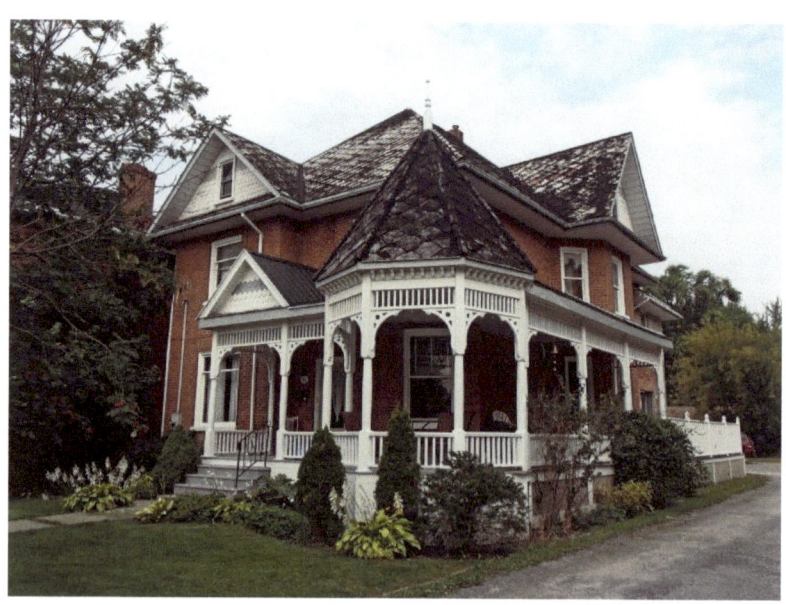

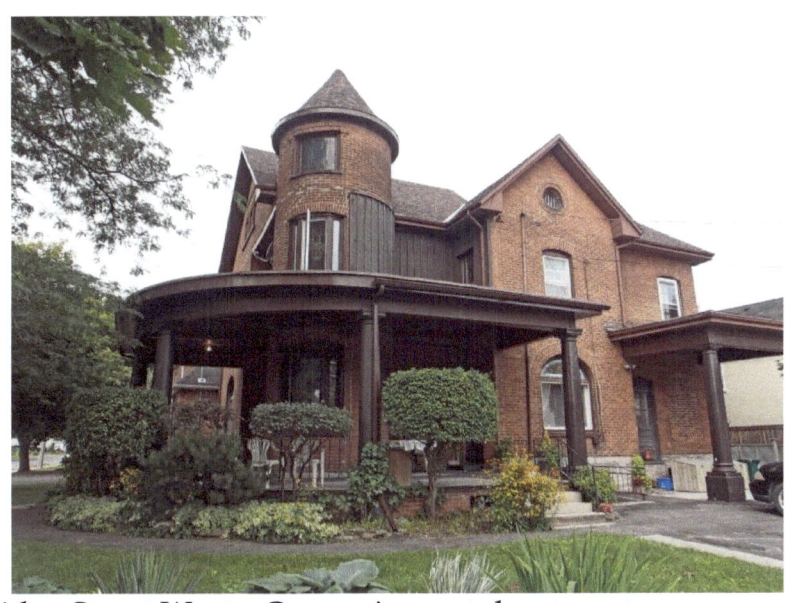

Bridge Street West – Queen Anne style – turret, wraparound veranda with Doric pillars

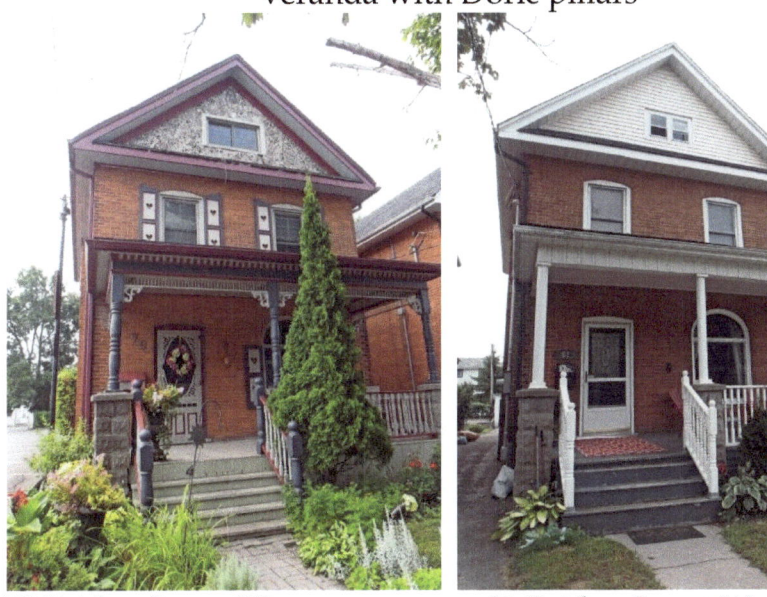

79 Bridge Street West –   81 Bridge Street West
                        Edwardian

– turned veranda supports
with bric-a-brac

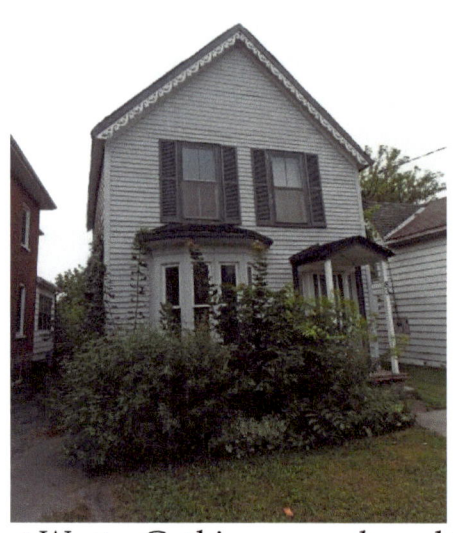

83 Bridge Street West – Gothic – verge board trim on gable, bay window

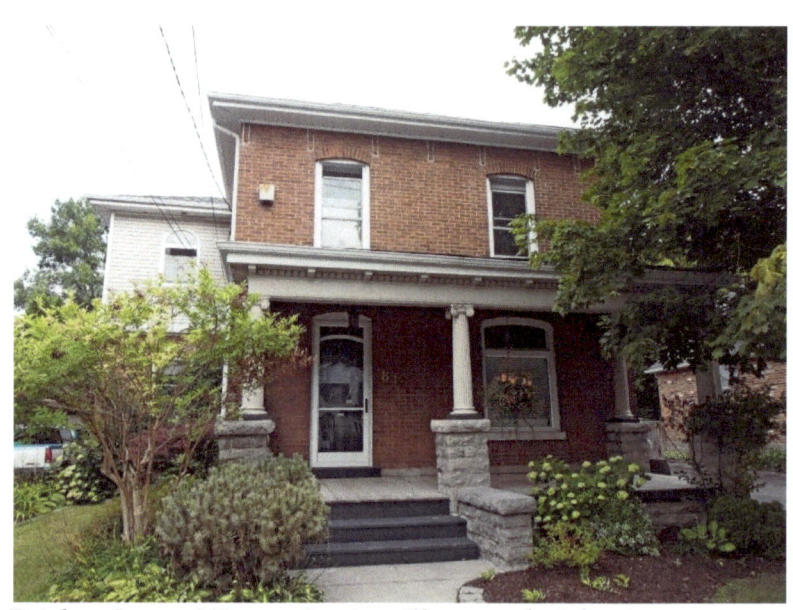

84 Bridge Street West – Ionic pillars on brick piers to support the veranda roof

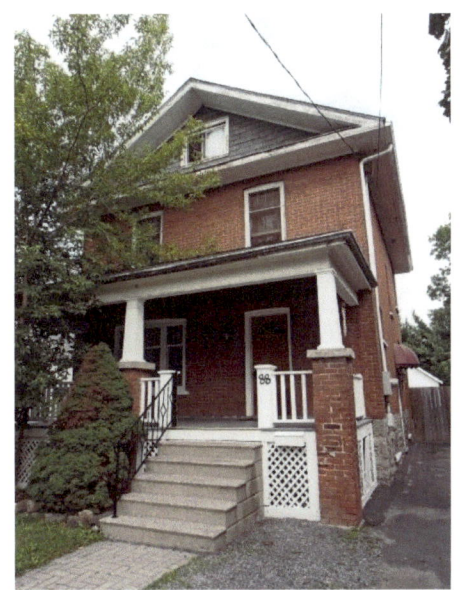

88 Bridge Street West - Edwardian

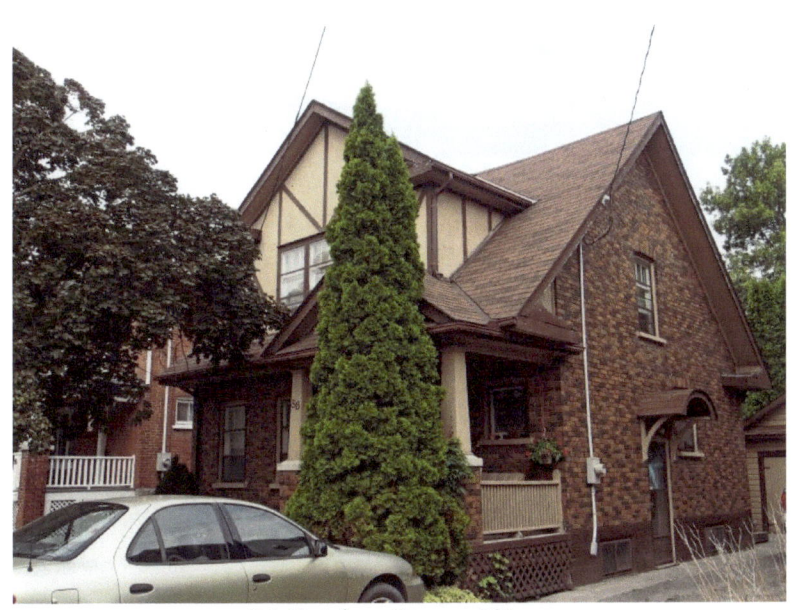

86 Bridge Street West

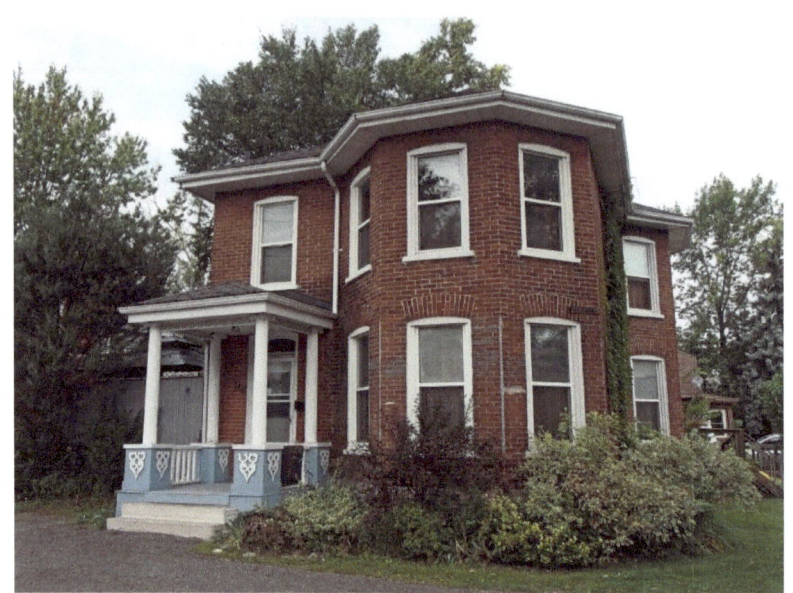

98 Bridge Street West

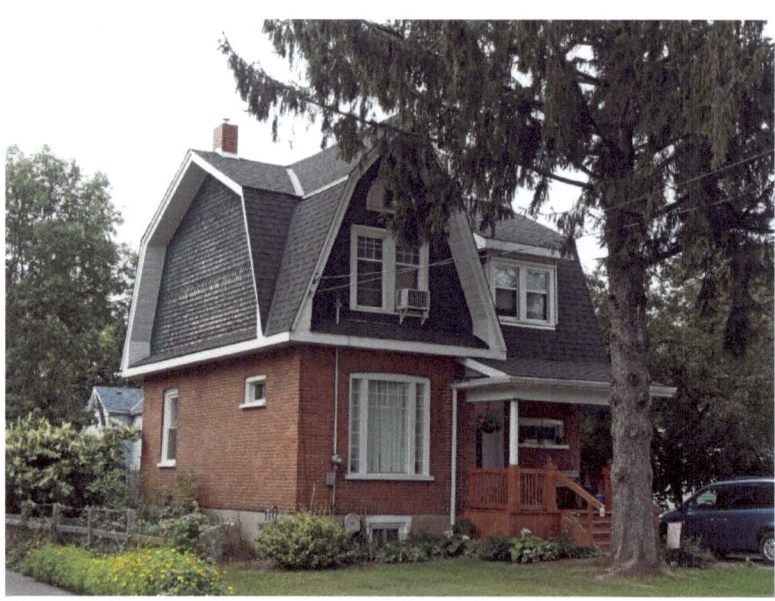

Bridge Street West – Neo-colonial style – gambrel roof

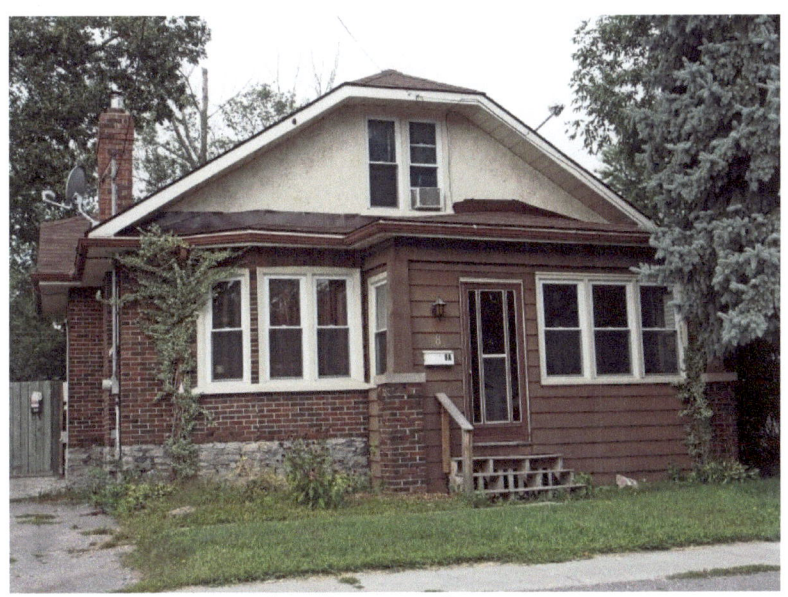

#8 – Ontario Cottage

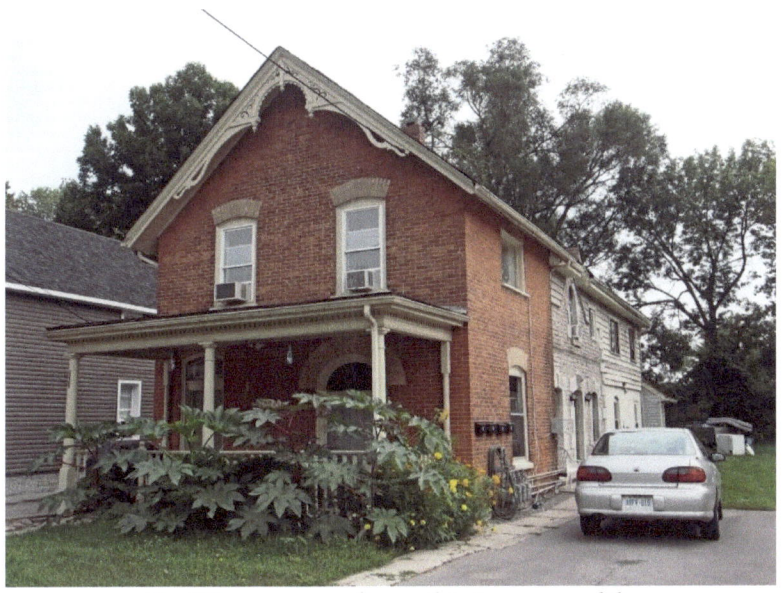

Gothic – verge board trim on gable

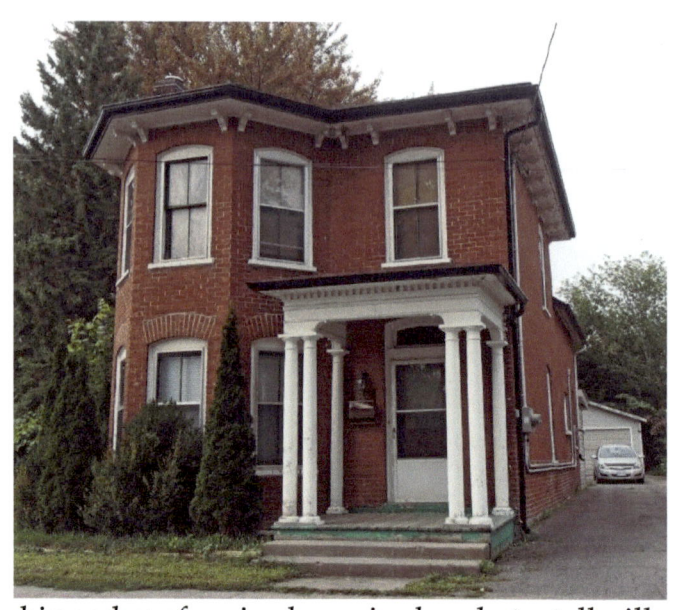

#34 – hipped roof, paired cornice brackets, tall pillars for porch supports

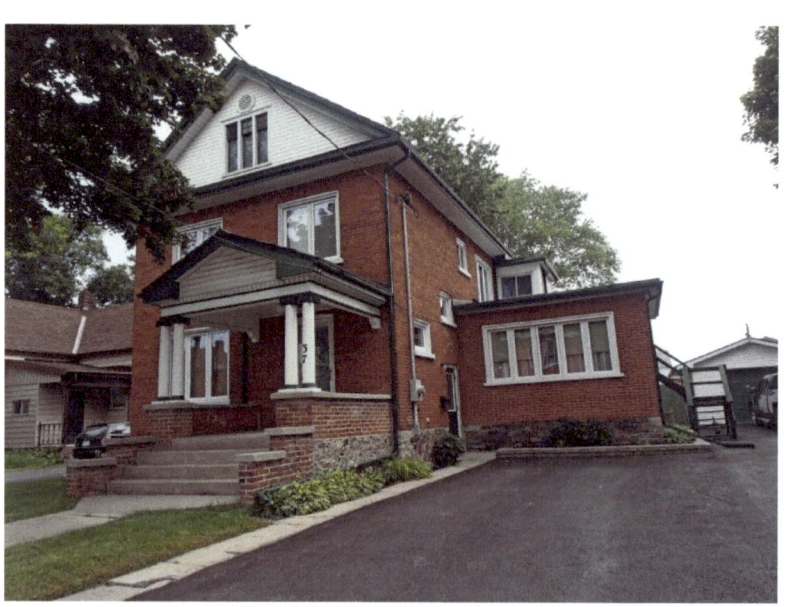

#37 – Edwardian, Ionic capitals, pediment

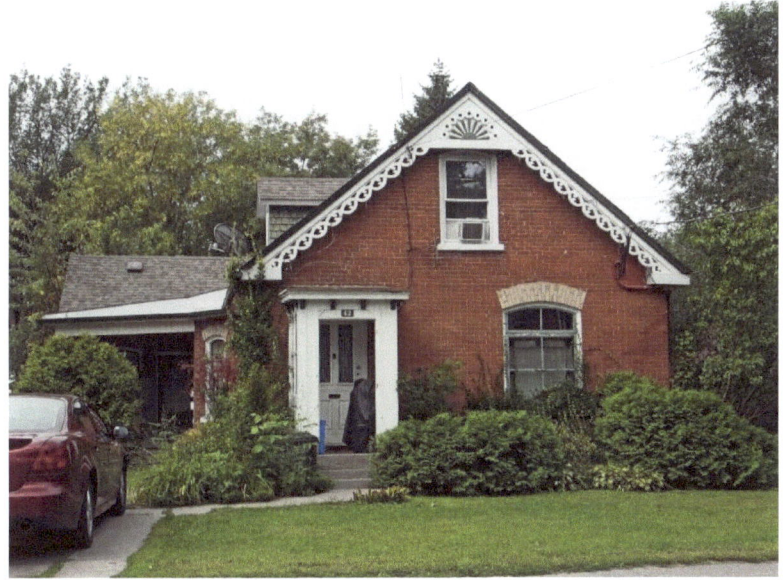

#42 – Gothic – verge board trim on gable, dichromatic voussoirs

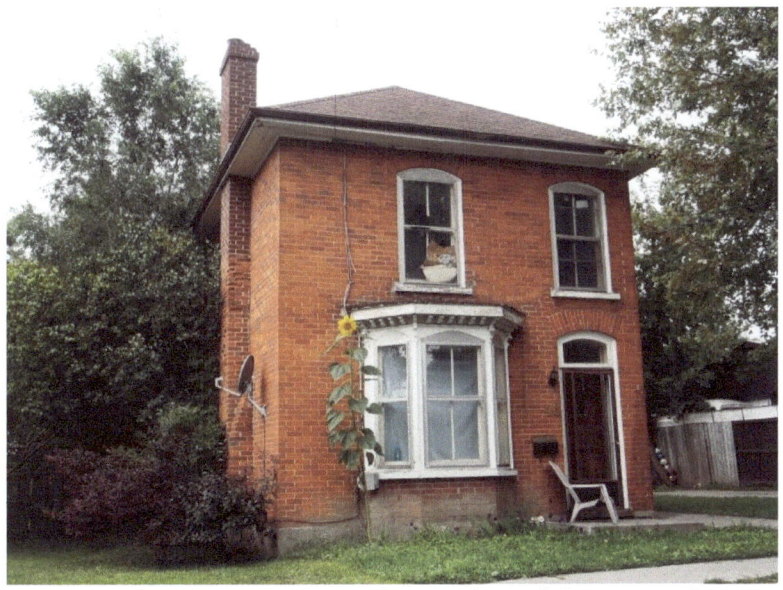

46 Bridge Street West – hipped roof, bay window

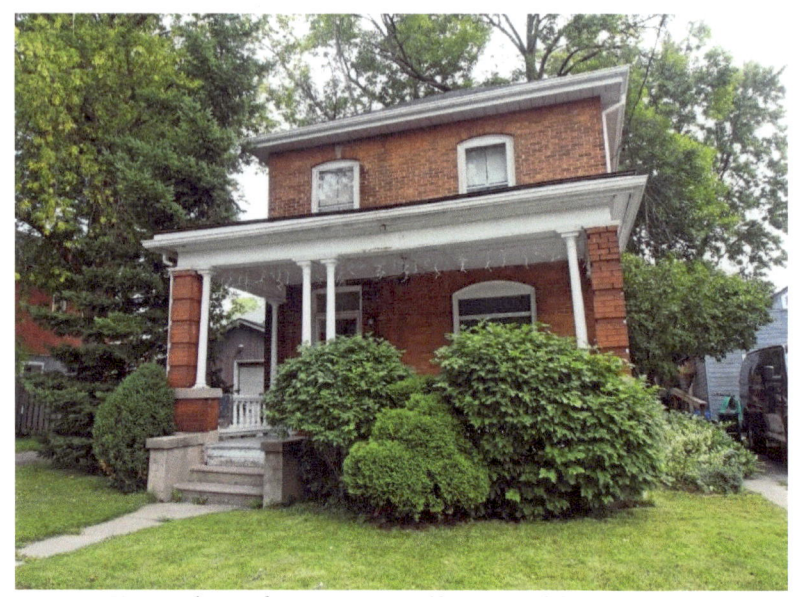

Hipped roof, narrow pillars and brick piers

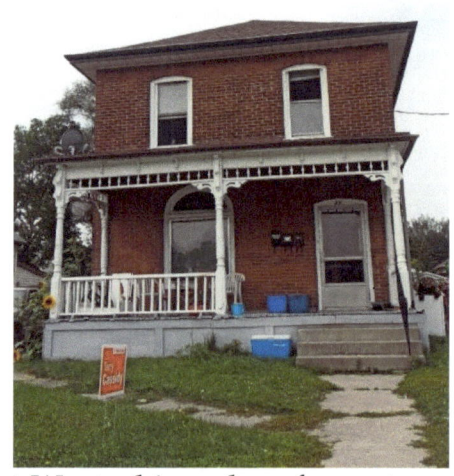

34 Bridge Street West – hipped roof, ornate capitals on porch supports, open railing

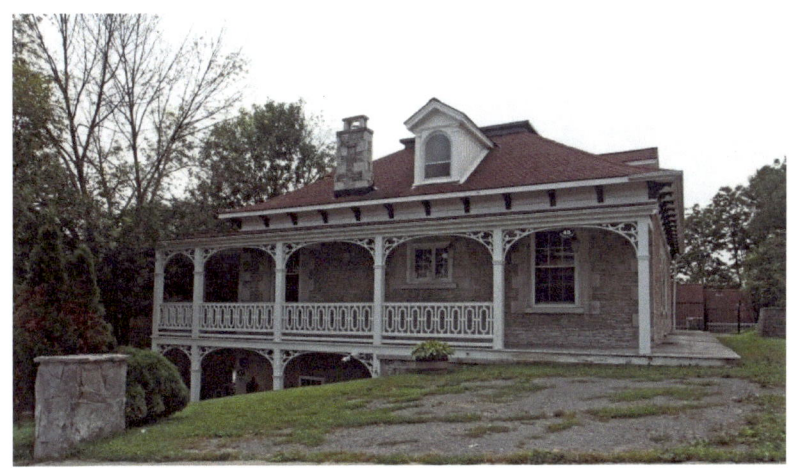

45-47 Bridge Street West – stone building, hipped roof with dormers and decorative chimney, cornice brackets, bric-a-brac on veranda supports

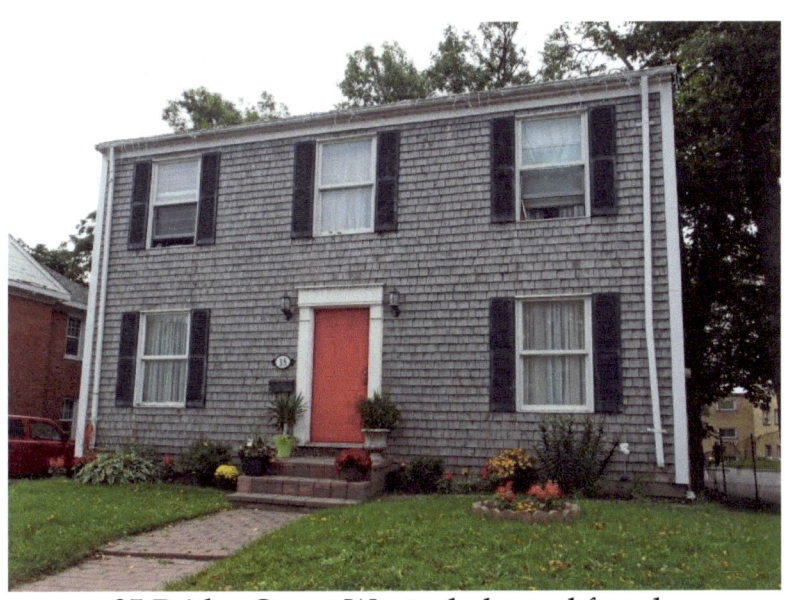

35 Bridge Street West – balanced façade

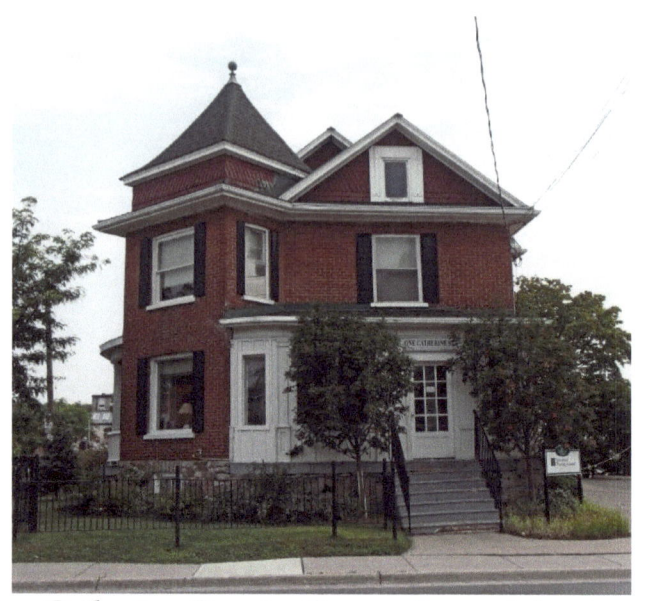

One Catherine Street – Queen Anne style - turret

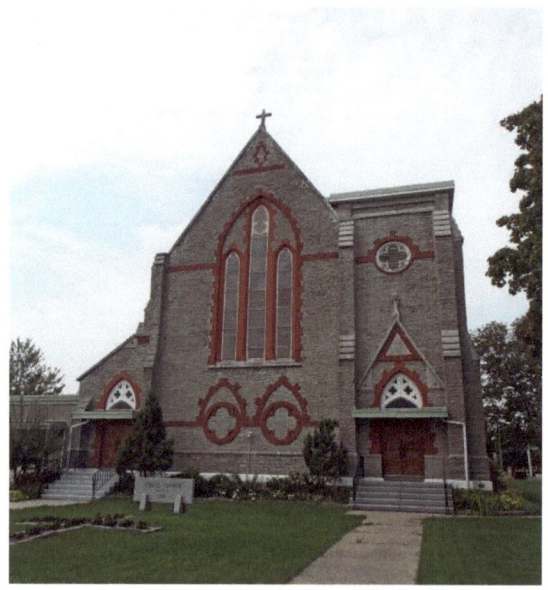

39 Everett Street – Gothic Revival - Christ Church Anglican – 1865 – buttresses, dichromatic brickwork

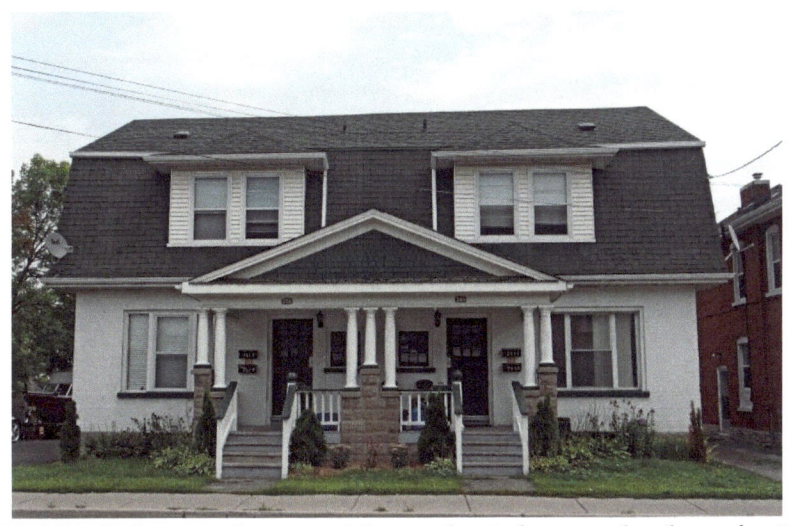

249-251 Coleman Street – Neo-colonial – gambrel roof with dormers, pediment, Doric pillars on cement block piers

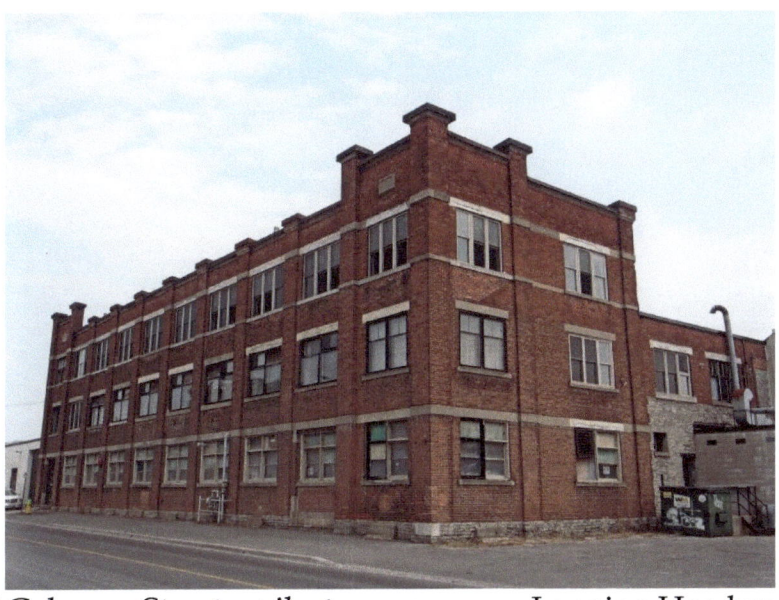

257 Coleman Street – pilasters, courses – Lanning Headwear – makers of all kinds of hats

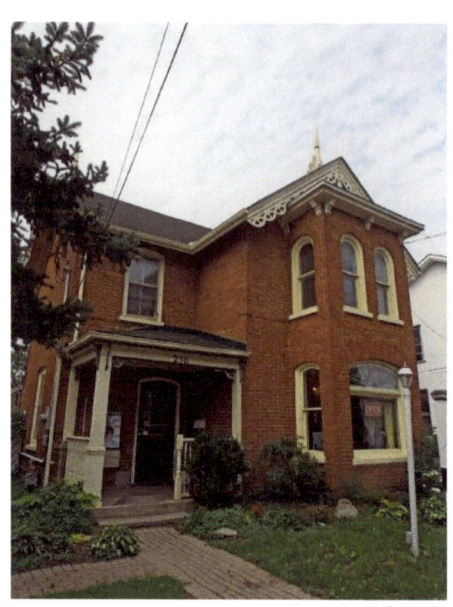

256 Coleman Street – two-storey rectangular bay with cornice brackets, verge board trim on gable

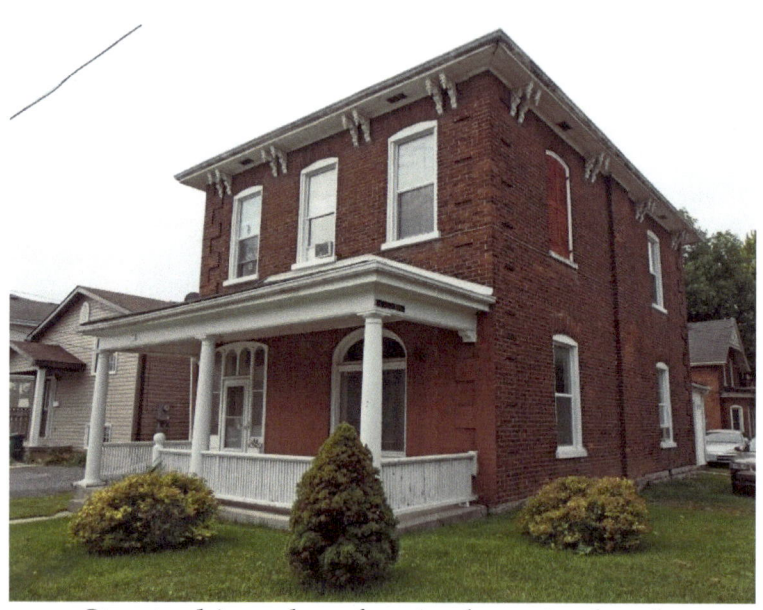

Coleman Street – hipped roof, paired cornice brackets, corner quoins, Doric pillars

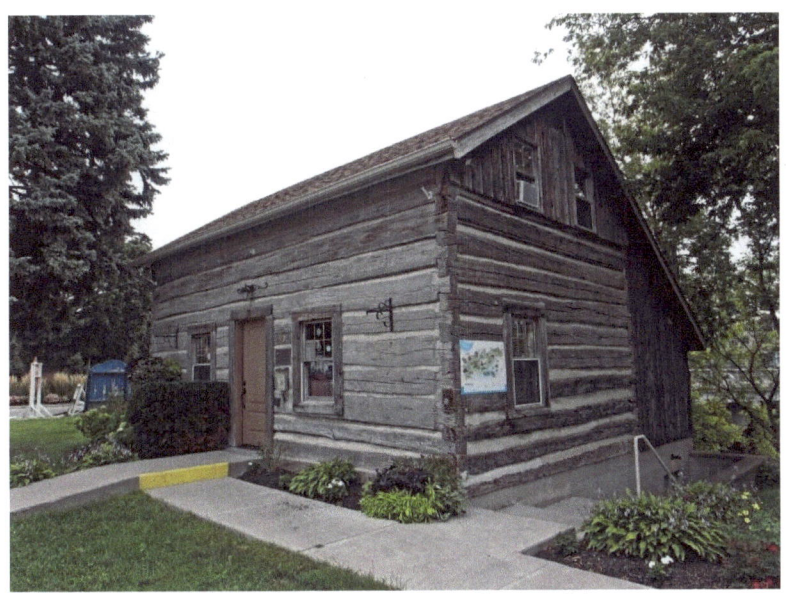

5 Moira Street East – log cabin

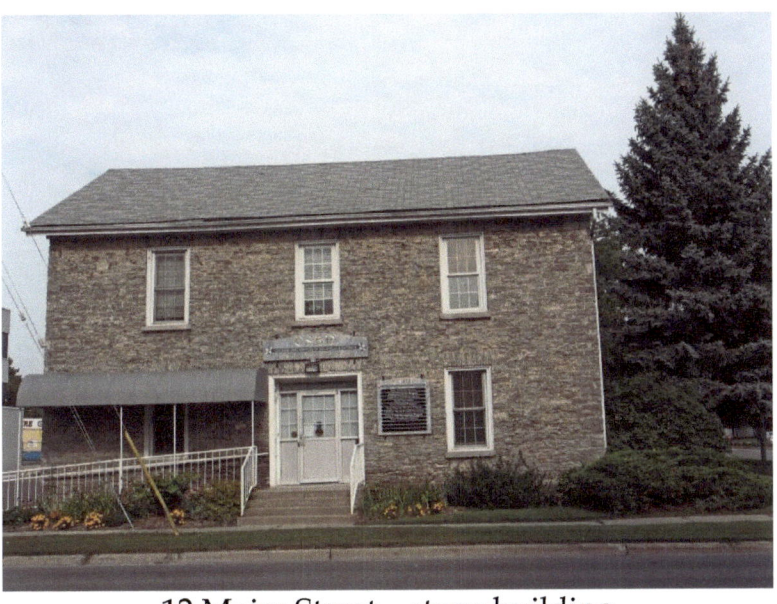

12 Moira Street – stone building

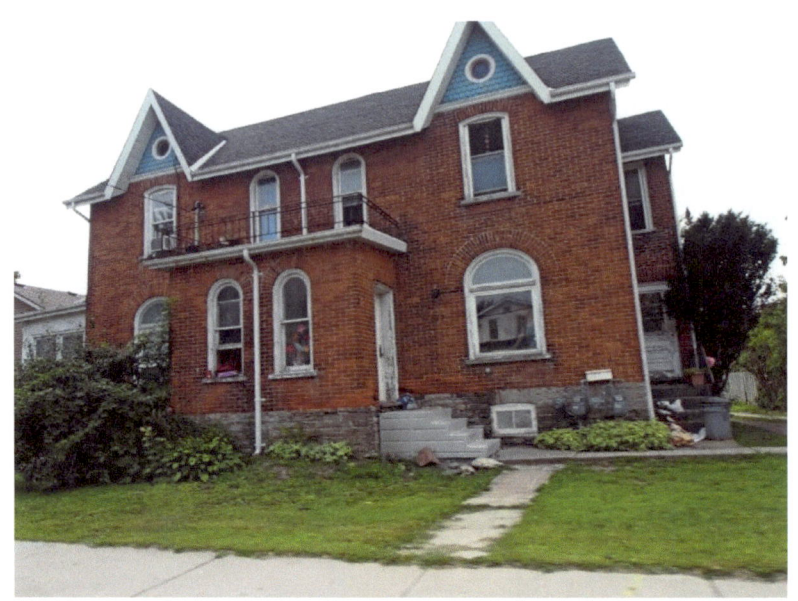

127 Moira Street – Gothic – second floor balcony above rectangular bay, voussoirs

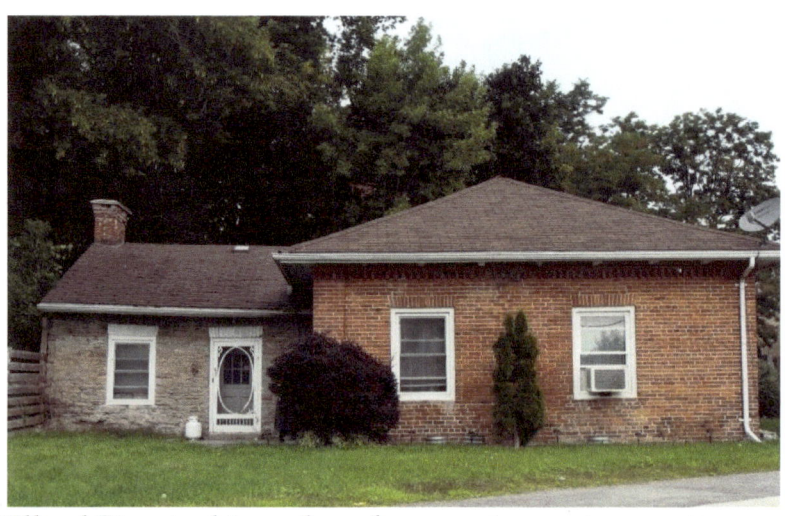

6 Willard Street – hipped roof – one-storey stone cottage with a one-storey brick addition

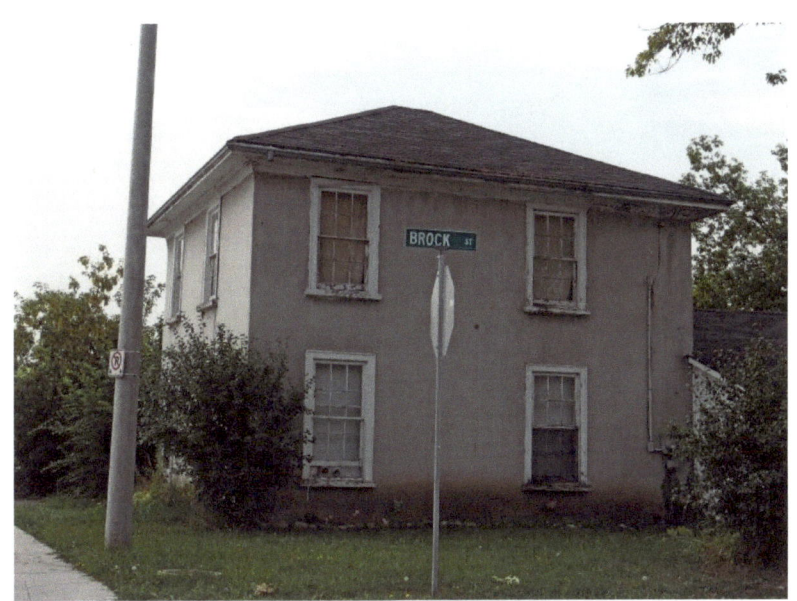

Brock Street – hipped roof

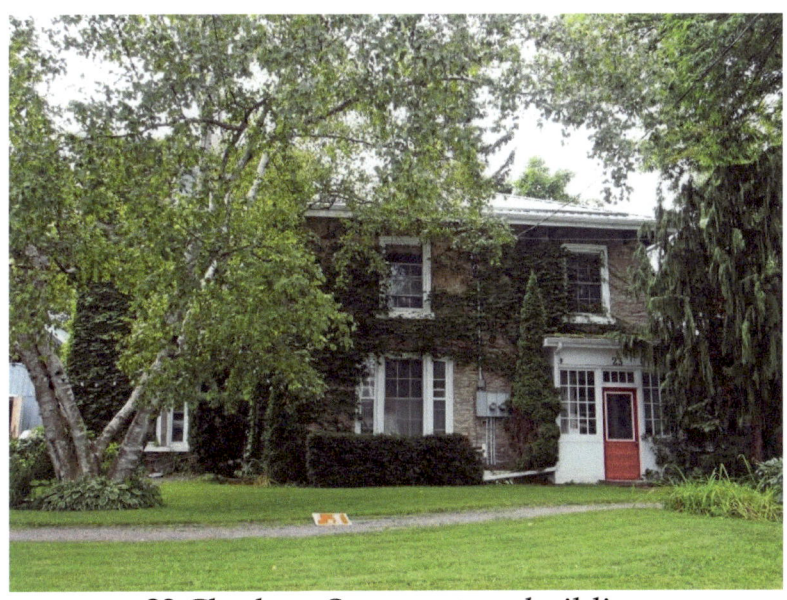

23 Charlotte Street – stone building

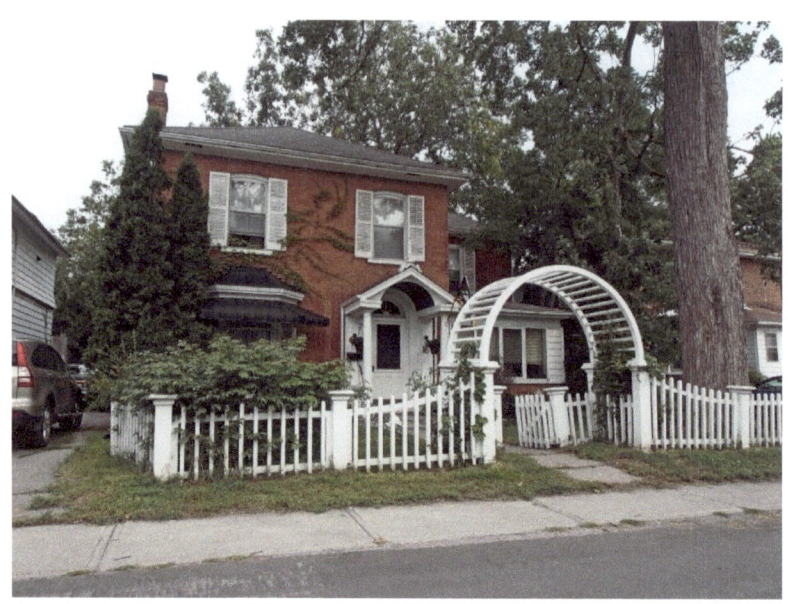

16 Charlotte Street – hipped roof, bay window, open pediment above door with transom window

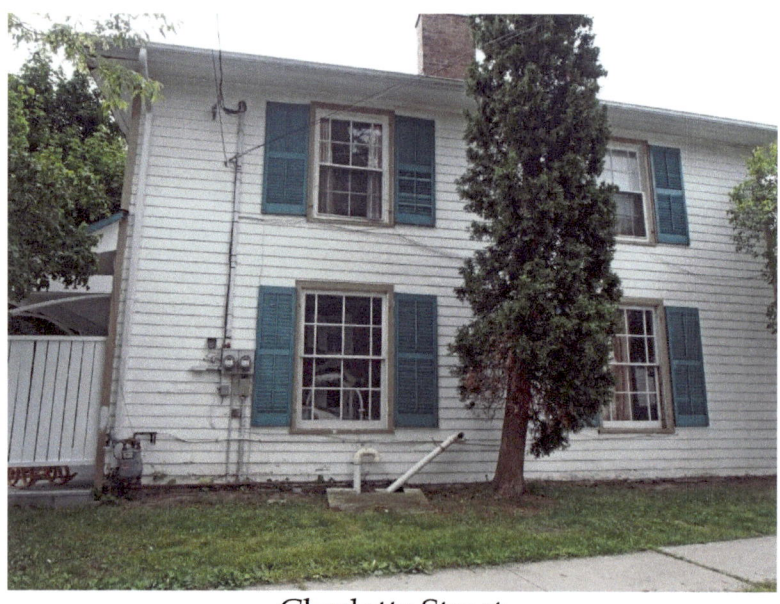

Charlotte Street

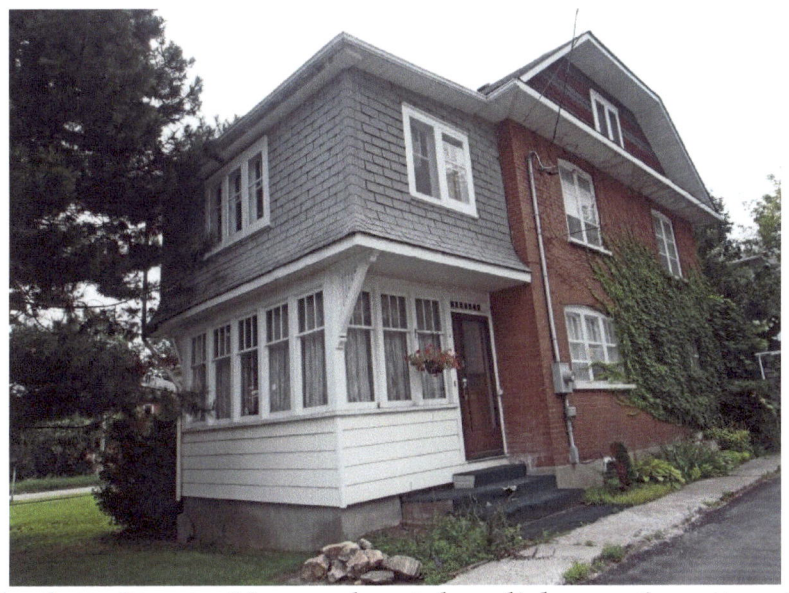

Charlotte Street – Vernacular style – dichromatic pattern in gable

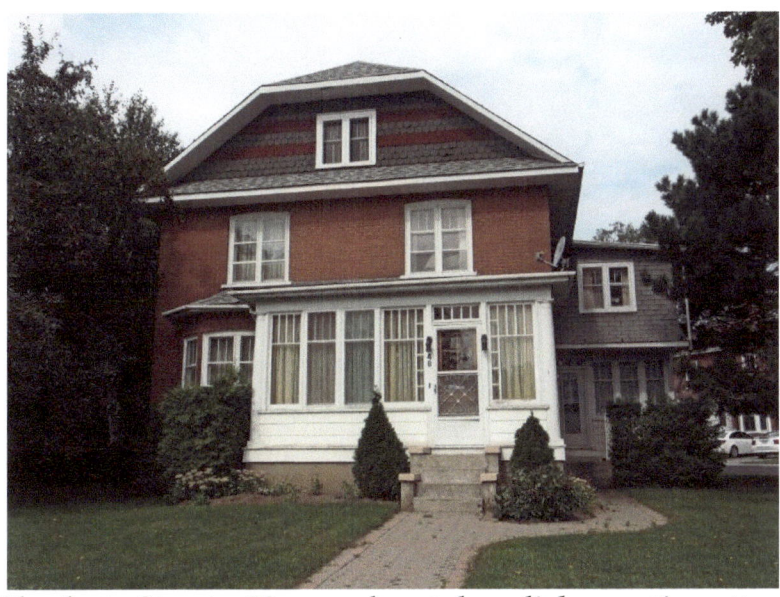

46 Charlotte Street – Vernacular style – dichromatic pattern in gable

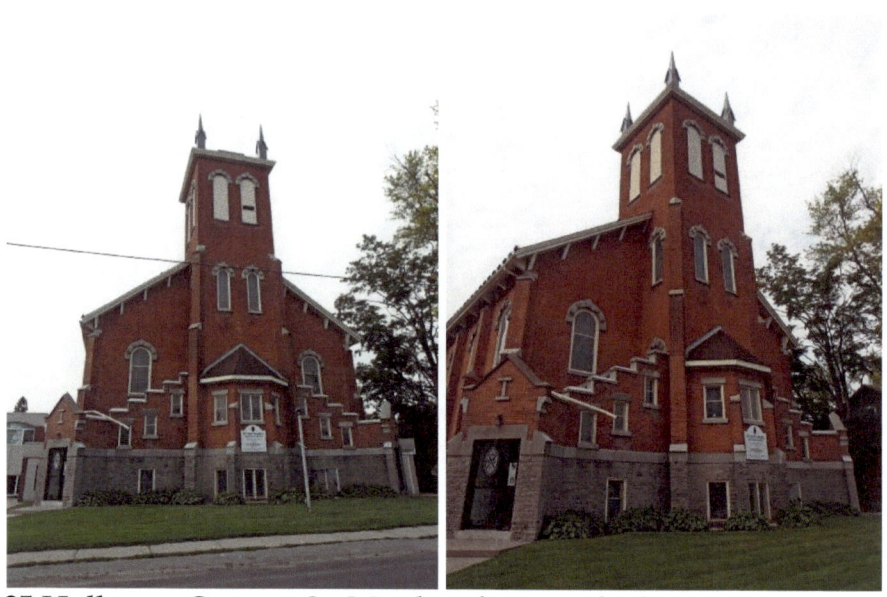

25 Holloway Street – St. Matthew's United Church – 1875-76 – Romanesque style, tower with finials, buttresses

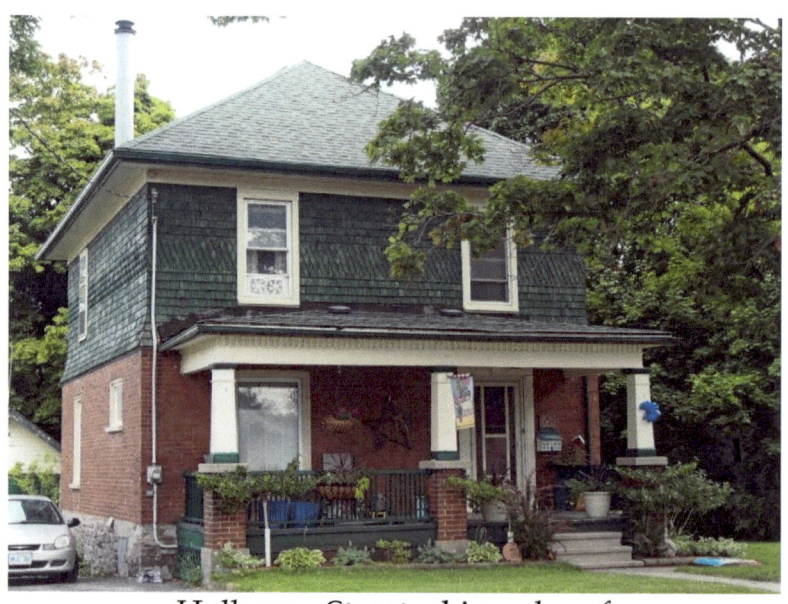

Holloway Street – hipped roof

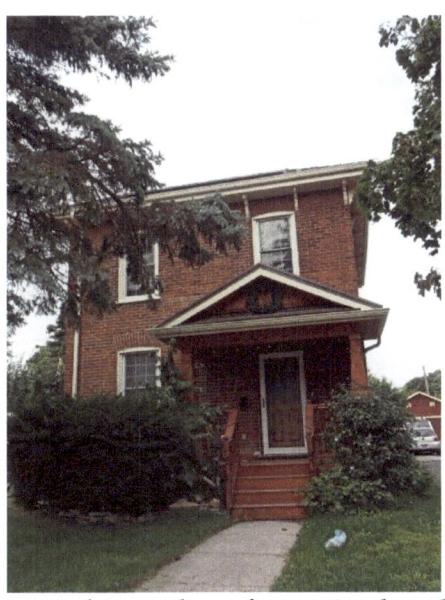

4 Holloway Street – hipped roof, cornice brackets, pediment

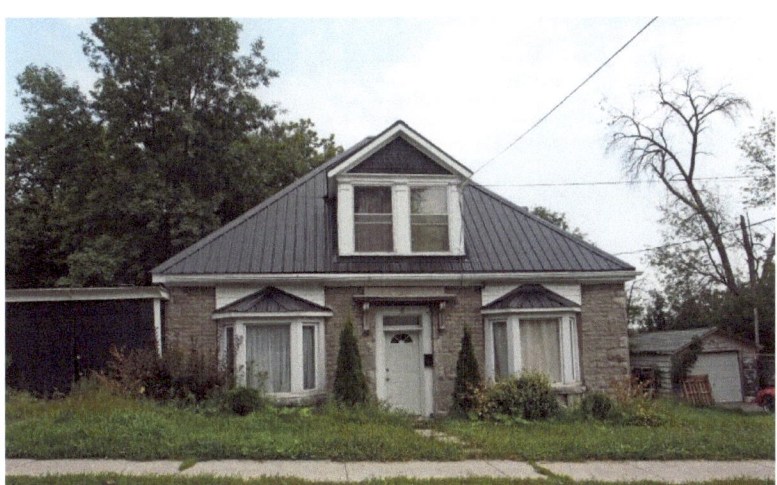

8 Hillside Street – stone Ontario Cottage – dormer, bay windows

Architectural Terms

Banding: Different materials, colors or textures used in horizontal bands along a wall. Example: 80 Highland Avenue, Page 30	
Bay Window: A window that projects out from a wall, in a semicircular, rectangular, or polygonal design. Used frequently in Gothic and Victorian designs. Example: 62 Alexander Street, Page 18	
Brackets: a decorative or weight-bearing structural element which forms a right angle with one side against a wall and the other under a projecting surface such as an eave or roof. Example: Hillside Avenue photo	
Buttress: a masonry structure built against or projecting from a wall which serves to support or reinforce the wall. In Canadian architecture, they are sometimes used for decoration. Example: 25 Holloway Street, Page 51	
Capital: The uppermost finish or decoration on a column. An Ionic column has a small base, a thin elegant shaft, and a capital composed of volutes which are carved whirls or twists that take the form of a scroll. Example: 84 Bridge Street West, Page 35 A Doric column is characterized by a plain column with no base, a shaft with twenty flutings, and a simple capital with a simple entablature. Example: 34 Forin Street, Page 11	 Ionic Doric

Cobblestone architecture: Refers to the use of cobblestones embedded in mortar as a method for erecting walls on houses and commercial buildings. Example: 114 Bridge Street West, Page 31	
Cornice: originally the wooden overhang of the roof. With the use of stone, brick, iron and steel, the cornice is any horizontal moulded projection at the top of a building. They can be very decorative. Example: 271 Front Street, Page 22	
Course: continuous horizontal row or layer of stone or brick. Example: 257 Coleman Street, Page 44	
Dentil Moulding: an even series of rectangles used as ornamental decoration in cornices. Example: 7 Forin Street, Page 7	
Dichromatic brickwork: the use of two colours of brick, tile or slate to decorate a façade. Example: 39 Everett Street, Page 43	
Dormer: (French for "sleep") a gable end window that pierces through the plane of a sloping roof surface to create usable space in the top floor or attic of a building by adding headroom. Example: 34 Forin Street, Page 11	

Frontispiece: a portion of the façade of a building, usually a centred doorway that is slightly raised from the rest of the building, usually has extensive ornamentation. Frontispieces are usually Classical in design with white columned porches. Example: 64-68 Bridge Street West, Page 32	
Gable: the triangular portion of a wall between the edges of a sloping roof. Example: 16 Forin Street, Page 9	
Gambrel Roof: a symmetrical two-sided roof with two slopes on each side; the upper slope is positioned at a shallow angle, while the lower slope is steep. It is similar to a mansard roof, but a gambrel has vertical gable ends instead of being hipped at the four corners of the building. Example: Mount Pleasant Road, Page 16	
Hipped Roof: a roof where all sides slope downwards to the walls with no gables. Example: 46 Bridge Street West, Page 40	
Iron Cresting: A decorative ornament along the top of a roof. Iron cresting was popular in the Baroque era and also in Italianate, Victorian, Second Empire and Queen Anne styles of architecture. Example: 44 Mount Pleasant Road, Page 15	

Keystones and Voussoirs: a voussoir is a wedge-shaped element used in building an arch. A keystone is the central stone that locks all the stones into position, allowing the arch to bear weight. A keystone is often enlarged and embellished. Example: 366 North Front Street, Page 25	
Mansard Roof: This style was popularized by Francois Mansart (1598-1666), an accomplished architect of the French Baroque period and especially fashionable during the Second French Empire (1852-1870). This roof is almost flat on the top section, with two slopes on each of its sides with the lower slope at a steeper angle than the upper, and has dormer windows. Example: 68 North Front Street, Page 21	
Pediment: a triangular section above the door or portico, usually supported by columns. The inside of the triangle is called the tympanum. Example: 70 Bridge Street West, Page 33	
Pilaster: a slightly projecting column built into or applied to the face of a wall for additional structural support. Example: 271 Front Street, Page 22	

Quoin: masonry blocks at the corner of a wall, often a decorative feature, usually larger or of a different colour than the rest of the wall. Example: 255 Front Street, Page 24	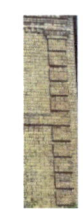
Sidelight: a vertical window that flanks a door, and is often used to emphasize the importance of a primary entrance. **Transom Window:** the light above the doorway, also called a fanlight. Example: 14 Mount Pleasant Road, Page 17	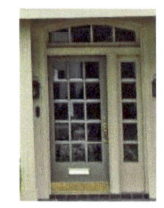
Tower: A circular, square, or octagonal vertical structure higher than the surrounding structure that is usually part of an existing building and is created either for extra defense or for a specific purpose such as a clock or a bell tower. Example: 68 North Front Street, Page 21	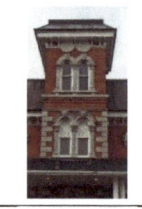
Turret: a small tower that projects from the wall of a building. Example: Bridge Street West, Page 32	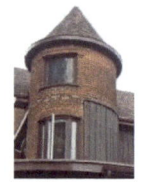
Verge board and Finial: also called bargeboards – hang from the projecting end of a roof and are often elaborately carved and ornamented. **Finial:** ornament added to the top of a gable, pinnacle, canopy or spire – a Gothic element. Example: 38 Forin Street, Page 12	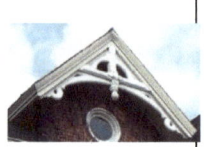

Building Styles

Beaux Arts: Promoters of this style sought to express the classical principles on a grand and imposing scale. Many of the Beaux Arts buildings were banks, post offices, and railway stations. The Ontario Beaux Arts style is eclectic mixing elements of Classical, Renaissance and Baroque. Often the designs have a temple-like façade, porticos with pediments, balustrades, and capitals in many styles. Example: 366 North Front Street, Page 25	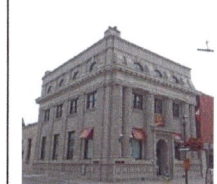
Edwardian, 1900-1930 – This style bridges the ornate and elaborate styles of the Victorian era and the simplified styles of the 20th century. Edwardian Classicism provided simple, balanced facades, simple rooflines, dormer windows, large front porches, and smooth brick surfaces. Voussoirs and keystones are used sparingly and are understated. Finials and cresting are absent. Cornice brackets and braces are block-like and openings have flat arches or plain stone lintels. Example: 79 Bridge Street West, Page 34	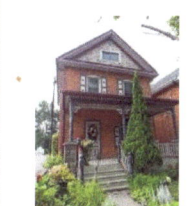
Georgian, before 1860 – This style began with the British King Georges in the 18th century. These buildings have balanced facades around a central door, medium-pitched gable roofs, and small paned windows. Example: 15 Forin Street, Page 10	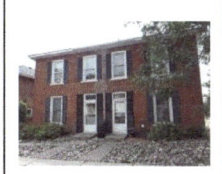

Gothic Revival, 1830-1890 – These decorative buildings have sharply-pitched gables with highly detailed verge boards, pointed-arch window openings, and dichromatic brickwork. It is a common style in Ontario. Example: 38 Forin Street, Page 12	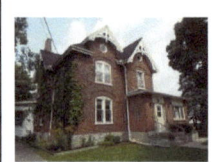
A **log cabin**, built from logs, was usually one- or 1½-storeys constructed with round rather than hewn, or hand-worked, logs, and erected quickly for frontier shelter. Log cabins were built from logs laid horizontally and interlocked on the ends with notches. The cabin was situated to provide sunlight and drainage so the pioneers could cope better with the rigors of frontier life. The pioneers chose old-growth trees that were straight and had few knots and did not need to be hewn to fit well together. Careful notching minimized the size of the gap between the logs and reduced the amount of chinking with sticks and rocks or daubing with mud to fill the gap. The length of one log was the length of one wall. Example: 5 Moira Street East, Page 46	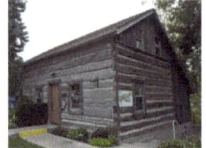

Neo-colonial (also Colonial Revival, Georgian Revival or Neo-Georgian) architecture seeks to revive elements of architectural style of American colonial architecture of the period around the Revolutionary War which drew strongly from Georgian architecture of Great Britain. Architecture from the 18th and early 19th centuries in Ontario includes a wide assortment of detailing and ornament applied to a design centered around the fireplace and the source of water. Structures are typically two stories, have a symmetrical front facade with elaborate front doorways, often with decorative crown pediments, fanlights, and sidelights, symmetrical windows flanking the front entrance, often in pairs or threes, and columned porches. Example: Mount Pleasant Road, Page 16	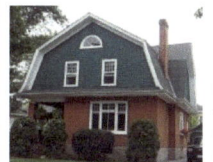
Ontario Cottage - one or one-and-a-half story buildings with a cottage or hip roof. The cottage roof is an equal hip roof where each hip extends to a point in the center of the roof. The hip roof has a long hip in the center. The Ontario Cottage is the vernacular design of the Regency Cottage which generally has a more ornate doorway and a partial or full verandah surrounding it. The roof can have a dormer, a belvedere, and generally two chimneys. Example: Forin Street, Page 13	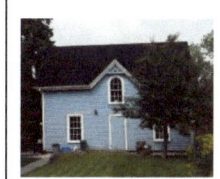

Queen Anne, 1885-1900 – This style is distinguished by an irregular outline featuring a combination of an offset tower, broad gables, projecting two-storey bays, verandahs, multi-sloped roofs, and tall, decorative chimneys. A mixture of brick and wood is common. Windows often have one large single-paned bottom sash and small panes in the upper sash. Example: 58 Highland Avenue, Page 29	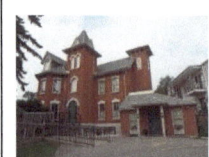
Romanesque Revival, 1880-1910 – This style hearkens back to medieval architecture of the 11th and 12th centuries with a heavy appearance, blocky towers and rounded arches. Example: 25 Holloway Street, Page 51	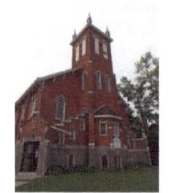
Second Empire, 1860-1880 – The mansard roof is the most noteworthy feature of this style and is evidence of the French origins. Projecting central towers and one or two-storey bays can also be present. Example: 80 Highland Avenue, Page 30	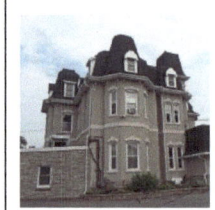
Tudor Revival – exposed timbers with stucco infill, multi-paned windows. Example: Highland Avenue, Page 30	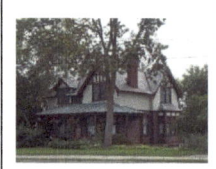

Vernacular/Traditional Mode 1638 - 1950 Influenced but not defined by a particular style, vernacular buildings are made from easily available materials and exhibit local design characteristics. Example: 46 Charlotte Street, Page 50	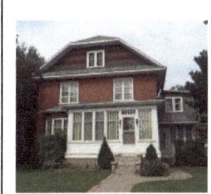
Victorian - In Ontario, a Victorian style building can be seen as any building built between 1840 and 1900 that doesn't fit into any of the other categories. It encompasses a large group of buildings constructed in brick, stone, and timber, using an eclectic mixture of Classical and Gothic motifs. Example: 68 North Front Street	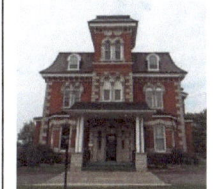

www.ingramcontent.com/pod-product-compliance
Lightning Source LLC
Chambersburg PA
CBHW040847180526
45159CB00001B/339